Early Learning Goals
for Children *with*
Special Needs

Early Learning Goals *for* Children *with* Special Needs

Learning through play

Collette Drifte

David Fulton Publishers
London

371.91
DRI

David Fulton Publishers Ltd
The Chiswick Centre, 414 Chiswick High Road, London W4 5TF

www.fultonpublishers.co.uk

First published in Great Britain in 2002 by David Fulton Publishers
Reprinted 2003
10 9 8 7 6 5 4 3 2

Note: The right of Collette Drifte to be identified as the author of this work has been asserted by her in accordance with the Copyright, Designs and Patents Act 1988.

Copyright © Collette Drifte 2002

British Library Cataloguing in Publication Data
A catalogue record for this book is available from the British Library.

ISBN 1-85346-936-X

Typeset by Elite Typesetting Techniques Ltd, Eastleigh, Hampshire, UK
Printed and bound in Great Britain by Thanet Press Limited, Margate, Kent

Contents

In memory of
Kiernan Frampton (1949–1981)
and
Spencer Frampton (1972–1981)

Acknowledgements

I should like to thank the following without whom this book would never have seen the light of day:

Jude Bowen of David Fulton Publishers for her patience and efficient and professional friendliness in supporting me through the writing process, Alan Worth also of David Fulton Publishers for seeing the book through the production process, friends and professionals who tried out the activities and made suggestions, the children's parents, and finally, but probably most importantly of all, the children themselves. Some of them feature in the case studies but, for reasons of confidentiality, their names and details have been altered.

Collette Drifte 2002

Introduction

'Well-planned play is a key way in which children learn with enjoyment and challenge during the foundation stage.' This quote from *Curriculum guidance for the foundation stage* (DfEE/QCA 2000: 7) should be printed in large letters and pinned to the walls of every early years setting. It is at the core of the philosophy of early years education and should be the mantra for all practitioners planning and implementing a curriculum for the youngsters in their charge.

The concept of play has been researched, analysed, discussed and argued about for some time. It has been addressed by psychologists, educationalists, medical professionals and academics, and has been explored in terms of history, behaviour, learning, education and culture. It has been used to promote various philosophies and approaches to educating young children and is even featured in some arguments for children's human rights.

This book does not aim to promote, defend or counter-argue any particular one of these ideas – the author leaves that to others who are more capable. It was written with the unquestioned assumption that young children do indeed learn best through play, through enjoyment and through having fun. Children with special educational needs (SEN) are no different in this and have the same rights to an appropriate curriculum that helps them to learn through well-planned play.

Many early years practitioners find themselves in a dilemma when faced with the pressures from head teachers or setting managers to cover the curriculum and produce measurable results. The desire to allow young children to direct their own learning through choice and 'free' play is thwarted by this necessity to 'do' each area of the structured curriculum. Research has shown that in many reception classes play is used as a 'reward' for completing work that is teacher-directed, often in the form of worksheets (Cousins 1999; Roberts 2000). Because of the pressures felt by the practitioner to cover the curriculum, the children are in danger of losing the opportunities that play offers, the valuable learning that arises from the well-planned play situation and the sheer joy that involvement in play gives to them. Practitioners need to examine their approach to working with the children and decide whether they are unconsciously placing too much emphasis on formal situations, and missing out on the learning opportunities presented by play. Are they essentially throwing out the baby with the bathwater? There are many chances during the routine activities of the day when play can be exploited by the practitioner to promote learning, and the final result will be measurable learning achieved in a fun and positive way.

Early Learning Goals for Children with Special Needs: *Learning through Play* offers the busy early years practitioner some strategies to help children with SEN to achieve through the medium of play. It has ideas, activities and suggestions, based on the philosophy of learning with enjoyment through well-planned play, for enabling the children to access early learning goals outlined in *Curriculum guidance for the foundation stage*. Because all children are unique, what they achieve and how they achieve it will also be unique, and no publication can hope to offer a strategy that will work for every child. This book, therefore, has suggestions and ideas aimed at the early learning goals, although for some children this level will be a future target and they will need to work through the stepping stones first. As with any learning, the initial stages and foundation work are crucial to the success of later work, and the learning by early years children with SEN is no different in this respect. It is of paramount importance that they are able to achieve each of the stepping stones in their own time, without being rushed through them in order for the practitioner to fill in a returns form or complete a tick-box section. It is crucial that they consolidate each stepping stone thoroughly before moving on to the next stage, and that the practitioner periodically checks and revises what the children previously learnt. The importance of the stepping stones stages cannot be stressed too strongly – they are vital to the children's success.

This book is based on *Curriculum guidance for the foundation stage*. Its chapters focus on the working and activity areas of a typical early years setting, in terms of each part of the foundation stage curriculum. These working and activity areas include the home corner, sand and water play, the music corner, the maths area, the book and story corner, the art and craft area (including malleable materials), table-top activities, and small and large equipment activities. Because each setting is individual, a brief description of each working area, as referred to by the author, is as follows:

- The home corner: the area of the room set aside for imaginative play, usually equipped with domestic play toys, a dressing up box, dolls and puppets, etc. It may also be turned into other imaginative play situations such as a shop, a hospital or an office.
- Sand and water play: usually confined to trays or large containers, each containing play sand or water. Water is often put into the sand for the children to explore the sand's changed properties. Both trays usually hold a variety of toys and small play equipment, to enable the children to experiment and learn through play.
- The music corner: the area of the room where the musical instruments, both home-made and commercially produced, are available and used. The children may be able to play with them freely, or at specific times, according to the setting.
- The maths area: the area of the room where the maths equipment and resources are available. It may also be the area where maths 'work' is done.
- The book and story corner: the area of the room where the main collection of non-fiction, story and poetry books is available. The display is usually changed regularly to ensure the children see a variety of books. It may be available on a permanent basis or only at specified times of the day, according to the setting. Often story or rhyme time is held here.
- The art and craft area: the part of the room where the materials for art and craft sessions are stored, including aprons, paint, brushes, easels, paper, pots, glue, model-making materials, clay, Plasticine, etc. It is usually where the art and craft sessions take place in order to confine wet paintings and gluey models to a specified area.
- Table-top activities: these include activities such as jigsaws, threading and sewing, board activities and games, drawing and writing activities, Lego and small construction equipment, card games, small people play and all activities carried out at a table.
- Small equipment activities: included in this category are bats, balls, quoits and beanbags, as well as larger blocks and construction equipment, play mats, hoops and other indoor equipment that is too large for table-top play.

- Large equipment activities: this category includes all outdoor apparatus such as swings, slides, roundabouts and climbing frames, and large indoor apparatus, including tricycles, bicycles and trailers, prams and buggies, soft play, ball pools, tunnels, parachutes and space hoppers.

A general book such as this cannot address every type of special need, difficulty or condition – the practitioner should consult the child's parents and read specialist books as part of her strategy of planning an inclusive programme for a particular child – but where appropriate and relevant, suggestions are made regarding the inclusion of specific SEN within the setting.

There are useful photocopiable activity sheets, which are designed to offer a quick and easily accessible follow-up resource for practice, reinforcement or consolidation of a teaching point. It must be stressed, however, that these should be used only when the children have grasped the specific concept being explored. Before any of the activity sheets are given to them, they should have had a great deal of essential concrete experience. This is crucial for children who have SEN, since they often find extreme difficulty in assimilating ideas in the abstract, and require lots of practical and physical examples that both illustrate a concept and give them the chance to explore it with a 'hands on' approach – often literally so. There are suggestions and ideas for using the activity sheets that can easily be added to, adapted or ignored by the practitioner according to her needs.

Each chapter features case studies that show how real people in real settings have responded to a particular situation involving a child with special needs. Early years practitioners are past masters at innovation and flexibility (they have to be!) and when faced with the problem of adapting their setting to include a child with a specific special need, they always rise to the occasion.

Finally, each chapter concludes with a list of relevant further reading and/or useful addresses. The idea behind this is to enable the reader to turn to the chapter dealing with the particular curriculum area she is interested in, and have all the information she needs within that unit. Bibliographies at the back of a book have a useful function in some texts, but *Early Learning Goals for Children with Special Needs: Learning through Play* has been designed with the busy practitioner in mind. Ploughing through a booklist at the end of a volume takes time; it is hoped that here, the inclusion of reading lists at the end of each chapter will ease that pressure. The book aims to be of use to all practitioners working in early years settings that include children with SEN, and also to students of childcare and early years education courses.

Further reading

Bruce, T. (1996) *Helping Young Children to Play*. London: Hodder and Stoughton.
Lindon, J. (2001) *Understanding Children's Play*. Cheltenham: Nelson Thornes.

1 Including children with special educational needs in the early years setting

This chapter covers:
- observation and recording
- planning and record keeping
- working with parents
- categories of special educational needs
- including SEN children in the working areas of the setting

In order to identify the needs of children with SEN, and then to plan and provide an appropriate and inclusive curriculum, the early years practitioner will have to observe the children, make assessments, liaise with the parents and the other professionals who may be involved, and then ensure that the setting is adapted to enable the children to access the curriculum.

Observation and recording

Careful and regular observation is the first step in gathering accurate information about the achievement level of the children. Some practitioners may feel that observation is not a priority, while others may experience a sense of time-wasting or even guilt if they are 'only' observing, but the importance of the role of observation cannot be emphasised too strongly. Staff in the setting should plan their system and methods of carrying out observations by deciding what type of observation sessions will be done, when, for how long, by whom, and why. Design an observation record sheet (similar to the one shown on page 11) that can be completed easily – it saves time and standardises the records within the setting.

There are two types of observation: Continuous Observation and Focused Observation.

Continuous Observation

This comprises short notes jotted down at any time during the day, forming a record of the child's daily progress and particular achievements. They consist of an account of what the child did and the related assessment statements, linked into the stepping stones or early learning goals from the foundation stage curriculum and/or the child's Individual Education Plan (IEP) (see Figure 1.1). They should be dated and initialled by the practitioner and put into the child's profile folder. Usually continuous observations are carried out and recorded by all members of staff in the setting.

> Clare Smith (4 years 3 months)   Model Making (Glue, scissors, boxes, etc.)
> 13.2.02 - 9.30/9.45 a.m.
>
>
> C. with Mrs. F. (teacher) and D.,P. & R. – C. pushes glue stick up to max position. Mrs. D. asks her to wind it back down. C. refuses and holds it in her hands. D. tells C. to help him with a box. C. puts down glue stick and holds the box for D. who puts glue on the box. When finished, C. squashes the box. D. cries and C. moves to other side of table. Mrs. F. tells C. to sit down. C. crawls under table and pokes at R.'s shoes. R. kicks out and complains to Mrs. F., who asks C. to help her with another model. C. comes out and stands beside Mrs. F. looking at the boxes. C. takes a box and cuts off a flap. C. throws down the scissors and the box. C. goes to R. and takes his scissors. R. protests. Mrs. F. asks C. to go to her. C. refuses and moves across to the Book Corner.
> (IEP target – to stay on task for three minutes)   S.C.

Figure 1.1 Example of Continuous Observation

Focused Observation

This consists of a fixed time, usually 10 or 15 minutes, where one member of staff records what the child does and says. Because events happen fairly quickly, she may make notes with key words and write them up properly later. Focused observation takes place less often and is usually carried out at an agreed time, to allow the observing members of staff to be released from their teaching. The number of focused observations per week, half term or term should be agreed by all the staff involved with the child, according to his needs. The practitioner records what was happening before an observed behaviour (Antecedent), the child's behaviour and language (Behaviour), and what happened afterwards (Consequence) (see Figure 1.2). She then makes assessment statements and links these in with his IEP and/or the early learning goals. The observation record should be dated and signed.

Before the observation, decide what aspect of the child's behaviour to focus on, such as his social and interaction skills, his language abilities or his level of understanding of a particular concept in maths. Filter out behaviours that bear no relation to the observation focus. So, for example, there is no need to write 'Charlie went to the toilet' if the focus is Charlie's ability to use a set of scales.

Write down observations either immediately or as soon as possible afterwards and be as objective and factual as possible to safeguard the accuracy of the observation – memory can be short or distorted when overtaken by other events in a busy setting. To be objective and factual, the observation-record must show only what happened, not the observer's opinion of events. For example, 'William took the blocks from Ahmed and then hit him' is more objective and factual than 'William was naughty and unkind towards Ahmed.' The first statement shows exactly what William did; the second tells us nothing except that the practitioner disapproved of what took place. 'Naughty' and 'unkind' are both subjective words, which mean different things to different people, and would tell the reader nothing relevant about the incident.

Use the observations to assess the child's achievement level and plan the next stage in his programme. Include samples of the child's work (paintings, writing, models, tape-recordings of his language, etc.) that illustrate and support the evidence collected

Observation Record Sheet

Child's name ....Clare Smith.. Age ....4y 3m..............

Date of observation ......20.4.02........ Reason for observation ....Social difficulties,...........

poor concentration

Antecedent What happened beforehand	Behaviour What the child did (an exact description)	Consequence What happened afterwards	Time
R. was playing with the syringe & funnel in the water tray. C. stood watching him.	C. took the syringe out of R.'s hand and moved away. No verbal communication by C.	R. demanded it back, called out to teacher and began to cry. C. ignored R. completely.	10.05
C. played with the syringe and then moved towards R. before trying to take the funnel. R. refused to give it to C.	C. hit R. and stood crying and demanding the funnel.	Teacher comforted R. and told C. that hitting is unkind. C. refused to play with a different toy. C. left water play.	10.06
C. moved to the table-top games and sat at the bead-threading activity. She ignored the other children.	C. tried to thread some beads - not successful. She turned the box of beads upside down and left the table.	C. moved to side area where morning snack was being made. She asked to go to the toilet.	10.07

Figure 1.2 Example of Focused Observation

3

in the observation-record. The samples should be dated and signed by the practitioner who was working with the child at the time (not necessarily the observer nor at the time of the observation), and should also include any relevant comments either written on the back or on an attached sheet of paper.

Observations will show what motivates, stimulates and challenges the child and should be used when planning the IEP and the teaching strategies. They are also useful for involving the child's parents in the planning process. By becoming aware of specific behaviours in the setting, the parents can watch for these at home and help to build up a fuller picture of the child. The spin-off is the closer liaison and cooperation between home and the setting, a crucial element for the SEN child's progress.

Planning and record keeping

A fundamental part of the planning process is the involvement of the parents and, where possible, the children themselves. (There will, however, be some children who cannot become involved in the planning process because of the nature of their difficulties.) Involvement means that they are very much a part of the team. Encourage the children to share in the recording and monitoring of their progress. Filling in achievement charts, showing the manager or head teacher an excellent piece of work, or putting merit stickers in a folder have a magical effect on children's achievement and self-esteem. It is crucially important not to use play sessions as a 'reward' for completing work or achieving a goal. In the early years setting, play must be an integral part of the whole learning process and should not become separated in the child's mind from 'work', and seen as something available only after 'work' has been done. This issue is discussed in the Introduction.

An IEP should focus only on what the child needs that is *additional to* or *different from* the setting's usual curriculum. Choose no more than three or four key targets, and write them on the IEP in brief and concise terms. Where possible and appropriate, link them in with the early learning goals or the National Curriculum objectives. Discuss the choice of targets with the child and his parents, and make sure they agree with and understand the aims of the IEP. Select the targets by working from the point that the child has reached, recognising what he can already do and deciding what the next stage of achievement should be, e.g. 'Johnny can now hold a ball and next will try to throw it a short distance.'

Next, decide on the criteria for success. This depends on what the goal is, but generally speaking you should agree on the number of times and the context in which the child should demonstrate that he has understood the concept or developed the skill. For example, 'Charlie needs to identify his name in written form': initially he should point to his name card among three others, twice a day for a week; then among five others, three times per day for a week; following that, he should point to his name on a large wall chart, and so on.

Fix a date for the targets to be achieved (usually in about three months, but this is flexible). If a target is achieved quickly, increase the goal; if the target is too difficult, reduce it. Work in small steps and if the child continues to experience difficulty, reduce them still further. This is crucial to remember, since the final target will never be achieved if the earlier skills have not been consolidated. Careful record keeping will highlight difficulties since a pattern of failure to meet the criteria will emerge over time. It is important not to assume that the child has retained a skill after he moves on to another one, so regularly check targets achieved previously. Don't allow the child to forget a skill through lack of practice – every so often, give him activities to jog his memory.

Plan the teaching methods and strategies carefully. While teaching strategies should remain relatively consistent, present the teaching point in a variety of ways. Children with SEN are often very context-bound. They may learn a skill or a concept in a certain situation and then be unable to generalise it. So, for example, they might learn that the plastic shape they are playing with is a circle, but won't be able to tell you that the wheels of a bicycle are also circles. When you discover a successful approach, try and stick to it and record this. If someone else has to take over, the records will prove invaluable since the child will continue to be taught consistently and successfully, and the replacement practitioner will also know exactly what to do and how to do it. If an approach seems to be failing, then change it. Failure can stem from a number of key factors, including: What (particle physics when Charlie still needs to recognise his name), When (at the end of the morning when the others are having a story), Where (at the back of the hall where the Daffodil Group is doing country dancing), How ('Death by a thousand worksheets' at the age of four) and Who (a personality clash with Mrs Bloggs).

Decide which members of staff are to be involved and the frequency and length of the teaching sessions, remembering that these should be flexible if the child is not gaining from them. Choose and record the resources to be used in the session, thereby saving a great deal of time in the pre-session preparation.

It is crucial to alter the parts of the IEP that are giving difficulty, whether these are the targets, the staff involved, or the time that the sessions take place. Professional integrity demands this; the child cannot alter his situation, so the responsibility for changes rests instead with the early years professionals.

Careful record keeping is vital. It may later offer important evidence of the difficulties the child was experiencing in the early stages of his education. It is also a vital piece of information about the What, When, Where, How, Who and Why of implementing the child's IEP, as well as providing the information needed to plan the next stage of his education.

Working with parents

A positive and cooperative relationship between the child's parents and the practitioners in his setting is crucial. This is nothing new to early years settings, but what may be unfamiliar to them is the involvement of the child's parents (and indeed, of the child himself) in the planning of an IEP, which, from January 2002, became a legal requirement.

The parents are the members of the team who know the child better than anyone else and as such they should be respected and valued as equal partners in the team. They must also be involved when the reviews of the IEP are held. They have the right to contribute to the discussions and the planning of the next phase.

Categories of special educational needs

The SEN Code of Practice (DfES 2001) recognises that children may have special needs as a result of:

- General learning difficulties – either in their own right or because of other difficulties.
- Physical or motor disabilities – conditions such as cerebral palsy, muscular dystrophy or dyspraxia.

- Medical conditions – asthma, eczema, diabetes and allergies (of food or other substances), etc.
- Emotional and behavioural difficulties – e.g. withdrawn behaviour, aggressive behaviour, or diagnosed conditions such as Attention Deficit Disorder (ADD) or Attention Deficit Hyperactivity Disorder (ADHD).
- Social difficulties – poor stimulation or delayed development through lack of experiences.
- Visual impairment – a vast range of sight problems, from the common condition of short-sightedness (myopia) to full blindness.
- Hearing impairment – a wide range of auditory problems, for example 'glue ear' or profound deafness.
- Speech and language difficulties – including the autistic spectrum disorders, Asperger Syndrome, speech dyspraxia, etc.
- Specific learning difficulties – in particular, aspects of the children's learning such as literacy or numeracy skills.
- General developmental delay – may be the result of many interrelated factors, including social, emotional, physical and personal.

Including SEN children in the working areas of the setting

The following sections give a few general suggestions about making the various working areas in the setting accessible to SEN children. It is by no means exhaustive and you will probably find many other ideas for accommodating your little ones, as you work together. More specific ways of meeting a particular child's needs will be suggested to the staff in the setting by the appropriate support services and outside agents.

The home corner

- Use persona dolls that wear glasses, have a hearing aid or are in a wheelchair, etc. to discuss physical disability in a positive light. Encourage the children to play with them amd to invent their own stories around them.
- Always store the permanent equipment in the same place so that visually impaired children will know where to find it. Ensure that it is replaced correctly at the end of the session. If you change the home corner's arrangement, involve the visually impaired children and make sure they know the new layout.
- Avoid using empty food containers and packaging made of polystyrene or plastic to stock the 'larder' in the home corner, since these may trigger a reaction in children with certain allergies.
- Keep shelves and cupboards, portable equipment and toys at an accessible height for children who are in a wheelchair or who may have to sit on the floor to play.
- Put dycem mats on the table to secure cups, plates, etc., for those children who have physical difficulties.

Sand and water play

- Always use the purest play sand to avoid triggering an allergic reaction.
- Put water and sand play trays on the floor for the children who work at floor level. Prop them up, if necessary, with big cushions or beanbags.
- Let the children with eczema wear cotton gloves while playing in the sand tray. Afterwards, check between their fingers for stray grains of sand.

- Let those with cystic fibrosis sit on a chair to play in the sand and water trays. Keep them warm and dry as far as possible.
- For the children with visual problems, put different scents into the water on different days. Have plenty of water toys that create different sounds, such as bubbling, whistling, trickling, splashing and so on. Vary the water temperature so that the children can feel the different degrees of warmth or cold.
- Have a variety of sand and water mixtures for the children with visual problems: some sand that is very sloppy with quite a lot of water in it; some that is firmer with less water; and some that is solid enough to make shapes or castles using different moulds. Have a good choice of moulds that the children can play with and feel.

The music corner

- Play relaxing and soothing music quietly in the room for calming children with behavioural and/or emotional difficulties.
- Have some instruments that make vibrations so that the children with visual or hearing difficulties can feel them.
- Use wooden floors for the same purpose, since the children will enjoy feeling the vibrations with their hands, bare feet, cheeks and body.
- Give the children with sight problems instruments that do not require vision to play, for example drums, shakers, bells, slide whistles and squeakers.
- Use Velcro bands to secure instruments in the hands of children who have physical difficulties, or alternatively attach the instrument to a band that can be tied around children's wrists.
- When making instruments out of 'junk', avoid using empty food containers, plastics or polystyrene if the instruments are to be played by children who are allergic to these materials.
- If you use sand to fill containers for playing, be aware of those children whose skin condition, such as eczema, may be irritated.
- Watch whether the children with speech and/or language problems join in with communal singing or reciting. Listen for the quality of their enunciation, the timbre of their voice or even, in the case of mutism, whether they have a voice – sometimes the condition is elective and the child who refuses to talk may sing.
- Use instruments that can be hung up, such as wind chimes or tambourines, so that children with physical difficulties can hit them using only one hand.

The maths area

- Stick magnetic tape or Velcro on the back of wooden or plastic numerals and shapes, so they stay on tilted or raised surfaces. Provide big shapes and numerals that are easier to handle for children with dexterity problems.
- Stick scales pans down with Velcro to prevent them falling off or being knocked over during use.
- Make numerals or two-dimensional shapes with textured materials such as sandpaper.
- Add colouring to water when exploring capacity, to provide a sharp visual contrast between the water and the side of the containers.
- Use dried peas or pasta pieces for weighing and measuring, rather than sand, to avoid allergic reactions or skin irritation.

- Make shapes out of different textured materials so that when they are tessellated, visually impaired children can feel where one piece finishes and the next starts. For example, a triangle made of sandpaper and another made of felt, tessellated in a square.

The book and story corner

- Read books and stories that feature characters with a disability (but not as the main character) and discuss the illustrations. Make sure that the book is explored together positively and in a way that shows sensitivity to the child with special needs, without being patronising. Leave the books out, together with some persona or disability dolls, for the children to play with and explore.
- Use visual props during story time. For example, puppets and dolls can represent the characters in the story. Encourage the children to perform actions or role-play the characters themselves.
- Provide books and equipment with clear images and bold pictures for the children with visual impairment. Check with their parents whether they can see line drawings better than photographs or vice versa.
- Make sure that books are on shelves that are at accessible heights.
- Provide books that incorporate communication systems such as Braille, Makaton, Blissymbolics (see Glossary).
- Provide books with different textures and/or incorporated noises that are activated by buttons.

The art and craft area

- Use a metal board and magnetic tape, or dycem mats to secure containers of pens or paint pots to the table.
- Give the children chunky brushes, pens and crayons for an easier grip, or wrap standard-sized handles in foam.
- Help the children who work at floor level to paint by propping them up with big cushions or beanbags.
- Adjust painting easels to chair height for the children with cystic fibrosis or in a wheelchair. Giving them long-handled brushes will help them to reach the paper more easily.
- When making models or collages, avoid polystyrene, plastic containers or old food wrappers that may contain minute traces of an allergen, as they can trigger an allergy attack.
- Use tactile materials for the visually impaired children – sandpaper, different fabrics, dried leaves, water, dry sand, wet sand, smooth and rough surfaces, 'sloppy' textures made from differing quantities of flour and water, etc. Scent the different colour paint pots with different perfumes.
- Use scents in clay, playdough or Plasticine for the child with visual problems.
- Put lentils, cornflour or sand into thick mixtures of paint for finger-painting by children with visual and/or physical difficulties.

Table-top activities

- Prop up children at floor level with big cushions or beanbags to do table-top activities. The whole group can play at floor level to include those with SEN in joint activities.
- Attach a tray at the correct height and distance to a supported child's standing frame so he can do table-top activities. Anchor the toys to the tray with a dycem mat.
- Base games and activities on touch, sound, sight and smell. For example, make a die with a small bell inside (Photocopiable Sheet 1), colour balls with fluorescent paint, or scent the Plasticine.
- Make a 'scent table', a 'hearing table', a 'feely table' with displays of things that appeal to different senses.
- Use tables with changeable heights or have a selection of different height surfaces. Position them near natural light, or good quality artificial light.
- Make sure that children sit at the right height, with their feet comfortably on the floor. Correct posture (i.e. where feet don't dangle in the air and knees aren't crushed beneath a table) is crucial.
- Provide chairs with arms for those children who need support and security in a sitting position.
- Make sure there is space between tables and other pieces of furniture to allow easy access and to prevent collisions.
- Try to keep furniture in the same place to give visually impaired children confidence in moving around the room.

Small equipment activities

- Use jumbo bats, balls and games equipment for catching, throwing and hitting.
- Use fluffy balls and bats with the 'hook' side of Velcro attached to the flat surface for catching; remove the Velcro from the bat for hitting. Wrap a strip of Velcro around both the handle and the child's hand if holding the bat is difficult.
- Give asthmatic children a whiteboard and marker pens (non allergic) instead of blackboards and chalk.
- Have a variety of balls: some with a bell inside, others with different surfaces such as smooth rubber or tennis balls, balls of various weights, balls that move erratically, balls with different smells made by soaking tennis balls in various scents.
- Leave out plants that have different scents and an assortment of textures for the children to explore.
- Use big, chunky crayons, pencils and brushes or alternatively wrap foam around the handles of standard ones to provide better grip.

Large equipment activities

- Fit handrails where there are ramps or steps.
- Make tricycles, bicycles and trailers accessible to the children. Put Velcro on the pedals and fix grips on the handlebars. Do the same for seesaws and swings.
- Check whether you need to administer prophylactic inhaled treatment before Physical Education (PE) sessions, to children with well-established exercise-induced asthma (see Glossary). Always liaise with parents and, where appropriate, medical professionals, regarding the administration of medication.

- For children with haemophilia, organise physical activities that involve lots of energetic exercise but very little risk of banging into obstacles.
- Keep the spaces between PE apparatus clear to help visually impaired children to avoid collisions. Use mattresses, big soft mats and, if possible, soft play apparatus.
- Keep the layout of apparatus the same so that children with visual problems can move confidently between areas. Pad any extruding corners or edges with foam. This is important for children who are visually impaired and those with haemophilia.

It quickly becomes second nature to anticipate and organise things to ensure that the SEN children are able to experience everything that is on offer. Even the other children become very clever in thinking up ideas for including their companions. Much of it is common sense and where there seem to be major logistic hurdles to jump, there is usually a commercially produced solution. As professionals, our responsibility is to make sure that the solution is found and that SEN children are as fully included as their peers.

Further reading

Inclusion in Pre-School Settings by Chinelo Chizea, Ann Henderson and Gabriel Jones (Pre-School Learning Alliance, 1999).
(A super book with lots of excellent suggestions and ideas.)
'Observing young children' by Margaret Edgington, *Practical Pre-school* **11**, September 1998.
Observation and Record-keeping: A Curriculum for Each Child by Ann Henderson (Pre-School Learning Alliance, 1998).

Useful addresses

Kidsactive
Pryor's Bank
Bishop's Park
London SW6 3LA
Tel: 020 7731 1435
minicom: 020 7384 2596
Fax: 020 7731 4426
email: ktis@kidsactive.org.uk
website: www.kidsactive.org.uk

National Early Years Network
77 Holloway Road
London N7 8JZ
Tel: 020 7607 9573
Fax: 020 7700 1105
email: neyn.org@virgin.net

Pre-School Learning Alliance
69 King's Cross Road
London WC1X 9LL
Tel: 020 7833 0991
Fax: 020 7837 4942
email: pla@pre-school.org.uk

Observation Record Sheet

Child's name .... Age ....

Date of observation .... Reason for observation ....

Antecedent What happened beforehand	Behaviour What the child did (an exact description)	Consequence What happened afterwards	Time

Photocopiable Sheet 1

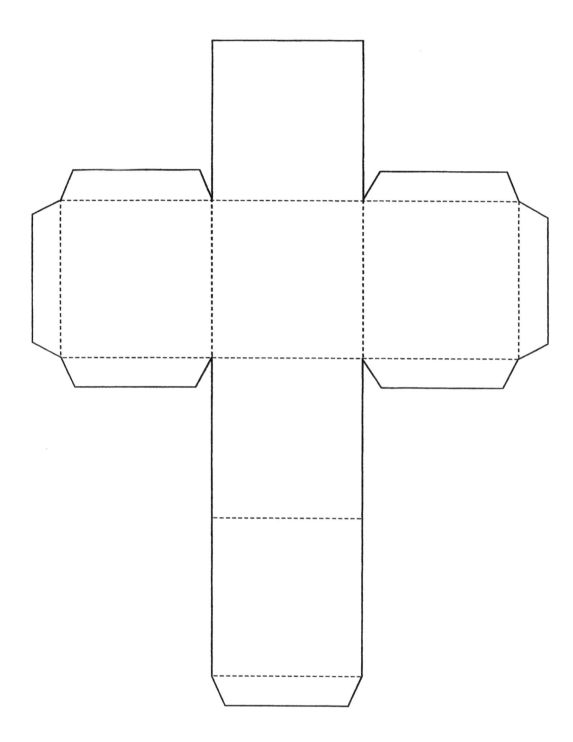

Use this sheet to make dice or cubes for tailor-made games and activities.

Photocopiable Sheet 2

Use an enlarged version of this sheet to make Snap cards, Pelmanism cards and other specific games and activities.

2 Personal, social and emotional development

This chapter covers:
- personal, social and emotional development and the special needs child
- personal, social and emotional development early learning goals and the special needs child
- personal, social and emotional development in the working areas of the setting

Personal, social and emotional development and the special needs child

Children's personal, social and emotional development depends on them being well adjusted with a positive self-image. SEN children's personal, social and/or emotional difficulties will show in their behaviour. They may be aggressive, withdrawn, uninterested in their activities, defiant, lacking in concentration, etc. Record what the children do and when, to see if a pattern emerges, e.g. are they always aggressive on a Monday morning? Are they usually tearful just after the lunch break? Discuss any concerns with the parents and share information in order to build up a fuller picture of what might be causing the problem.

Behaviour management

There are several fundamental points behind the successful management of the child's behaviour.
1. Always be consistent. If something isn't allowed, say 'No' **every** time. Make sure everyone in the setting does the same.
2. Be a good role model.
3. Set some rules for everyone to stick to (see below). The children feel secure when they know what's expected of them.
4. Never physically punish children or humiliate them, particularly in front of others. 'Sin bins', 'naughty seats' or sarcastic comments should never be used.
5. Use positive terms when speaking to the children about their behaviour, e.g. 'Charlie, come and sit beside me to look at this book' rather than 'Charlie, don't wander around the room.'
6. Explain gently to the children what you want them to do and why, in specific terms such as 'Charlie, I'd like you to come and sit beside me to look at this book because the others can't hear the story when you make that noise.'
7. Ignore unwanted behaviour as far as possible, and give lots of praise and attention when the children do behave as you want them to.

Some appropriate strategies

Draw up a behaviour management policy
Be sure to involve everyone connected with the setting, including the children where possible, as ownership and commitment mean the policy is more likely to work. Start by deciding on 'house rules' for the children to follow and practitioners to implement (see below). Agree on methods for modifying children's behaviour and decide when to review the policy.

Set some house rules
Establish some rules for the children to follow such as 'Be kind to everyone', 'Move around carefully' and 'Keep our room tidy'. Come up with a separate set for practitioners to implement, which might, for example, allow outside play only with adult supervision, allow shouting only outside, or limit the number of children in the water play area to four at any time.

Agree a behaviour modification programme
Ensure that you devise a programme that will allow you to observe and identify the undesired behaviour, and to recognise triggers so that as many of them as possible can be removed, e.g. by rearranging the room or groupings. Decide on a programme that agrees to ignore the undesired behaviour and focuses instead on the behaviour to be encouraged. The positive rewards that will be used to reinforce the desired behaviour should also be identified at this stage, e.g. praise, treats or stickers.

Adopt positive principles
It is important to recognise children's 'warning signs', which often pre-empt unwanted behaviour, and to act quickly to distract those involved or remove them from the situation. Have a 'quiet corner' where the children can sit to calm themselves when they feel upset and make sure this is regarded as a pleasant place. Encourage the children to talk to you when they are upset and try to maintain a calm atmosphere that is unhurried yet stimulating. It is worthwhile to establish a regular routine where the daily events, such as drinks and biscuits, always happen at the same time.

Concentration

Observe what a child enjoys doing most and how long he stays on task, then observe his concentration span with other activities. Beginning with his favourite activity, gradually increase the time, adding 10, 15, 20, 30 seconds and so on, to his maximum span. Praise him for concentrating so well and then move to another activity before he becomes uninterested.

When the child stays on task for longer, tackle other activities in the same way. Always finish an activity as soon as there are signs of restlessness, and be sure to conclude with praise for the child's effort.

Personal, social and emotional development early learning goals and the special needs child

SEN children should aim for the same goals as all children, but they may take longer to achieve them. They need to:

- establish positive and trusted relationships with everyone in the setting, and adults from outside, e.g. parents or external agents;
- experience working alone, in a one-to-one situation with an adult, with the other children in small groups, in large groups and in a whole-setting situation, and to feel comfortable in each of these;
- experiment and take part in activities that will help their personal and social development;
- experience literature, resources and equipment that will interest, excite and stimulate them;
- develop self-help skills and independence through involvement in activities and sessions that include a degree of responsibility and choice.

Personal, social and emotional development in the working areas of the setting

The home corner

Use the home corner to:

- help the children with language difficulties to play imaginatively; plan activities that are based on their real-life situations and experiences;
- help the child with an autistic spectrum disorder who compulsively or obsessively sorts, orders and lines up the toys and equipment; gently intervene and help the child to develop more normal play skills by modelling first and then helping him to follow suit;
- include the SEN children in imaginative play in a group situation, e.g. setting a dinner place for a physically disabled child, even if he finds holding cutlery difficult;
- encourage the children who have motor difficulties to practise self-help skills by dressing up;
- help the children with ADHD or ADD to develop social skills – their main area of difficulty – through social play.

Case study
Susie, Jason and Clare are playing in the home corner with Benny who has Asperger Syndrome. He watches Susie put a ribbon on a cuddly toy dog's snout, as a 'Gentle Leader'.

> Benny: You shouldn't do that. That's cruel. You shouldn't do that to the dog.

> Susie: It's not cruel. It stops him from pulling me over when we go for a walk. My dog's got one at home. He pulls my mum if he doesn't wear it.

> (Benny turns to Jason.)

> Benny: Susie's put the thing on the dog to stop him pulling her over. It's not cruel.

Benny listened to Susie's explanation and then changed his mind about what she was doing. His interaction with her enabled him to see another person's point of view and acknowledge that his original opinion could be altered.

Handy hints

Help the children to plan and change the home corner for communal play, e.g. a bus or a hair salon, including children with social difficulties in the group. Encourage imaginative play that involves SEN children, supporting them if necessary in their interactions with the others.

Play with the children who have autistic spectrum disorders in a one-to-one situation initially, remembering that at first they might play alongside as opposed to with you. Invite them to join in with whatever you do, gradually encouraging them to use the equipment and toys appropriately. As the children gain confidence, invite another child to join you. Gradually increase the group. This may take some time to achieve.

Early learning goals and the home corner
Time spent in the home corner can focus on the following early learning goals:
- Form good relationships with adults and peers.
- Dress and undress independently and manage their own personal hygiene.
- Work as part of a group or class, taking turns and sharing fairly, understanding that there need to be agreed values and codes of behaviour for groups of people, including adults and children, to work together harmoniously.

Sand and water play

During sand and water play:

- encourage the children to put on and take off waterproof overalls by themselves, to practise self-help skills. Washing and drying their hands at the end takes this a stage further. By helping others to put on their overalls, children will also be practising their social skills;

- have joint activities, e.g. building a giant sand castle or watercourse, which involve the children in communal play, discussions and cooperative decisions – all valuable experiences in social interaction;
- involve the children in tidying and cleaning up spillages of water or sand, explaining that this is to make sure that the area is safe and pleasant for the next group of children;
- include the children whose hearing is impaired in pair or group play. They may need help to develop their imaginative and/or symbolic play, and cooperative activities here will support this.

Handy hints

☞ Use arguments about sharing water or sand toys as an opportunity to help children with social and/or emotional difficulties to negotiate and take turns. For example, encourage partners to agree a solution such as having three 'gos' with the toy and then handing it over.

☞ During sand and water play, encourage the group to share their ideas and experiences. Encourage children who have sensory impairment to talk about sand and water play experiences in terms of their other senses, thus ensuring that they are included in the general discussion.

▓ *Early learning goals and sand and water play*

Time spent in sand and water play can focus on the following early learning goals:

- Be confident to try new activities, initiate ideas and speak in a familiar group.
- Have a developing awareness of their own needs, views and feelings, and be sensitive to the needs, views and feelings of others.
- Consider the consequences of their words and actions for themselves and others.
- Dress and undress independently and manage their own personal hygiene.

The music corner

Music is perfect for:

- cooperative play – when SEN children play instruments, in pairs or small groups, they learn to work harmoniously (no pun intended!);
- trying out new ideas – some SEN children may be diffident about meeting new challenges, but music is a fun way to help overcome this;
- personal development – most SEN children benefit hugely from exploring music (music therapy is acknowledged as being a positive approach) and many discover talents they were unaware of.

Handy hints

When composing music together, put the group into pairs, including the SEN children, to explore and play the same instrument(s), so giving them the support of their peers as well as the experience of cooperation.

Encourage children to experiment with new 'non-musical' objects to see how they can turn them into an instrument and play them, e.g. a paintbrush and a tin, the floor and bubble wrap. If the children perceive this as a positive and fun activity, they will be stimulated to try new ideas.

Early learning goals and the music corner

Time spent in the music corner can focus on the following early learning goals:

- Continue to be interested, excited and motivated to learn.
- Be confident to try new activities, initiate ideas and speak in a familiar group.
- Maintain attention, concentrate, and sit quietly when appropriate.

The maths area

Use maths to:

- include the SEN children in pair work through games, e.g. play 'shape partners' in which you give each child a shape that can be matched, tessellated or joined to make another, and challenge them to find their 'shape partner';
- play cooperative counting games that include children with SEN, e.g. working in pairs or small groups, how many large balls can the children throw into a basket?
- provide group activities, involving the SEN children, e.g. each child in the group takes turns to feel a stone and a feather before the group makes a joint decision about which is heavier.

Handy hints

Make sure that storage areas are labelled clearly with the maths equipment's name and a picture or sample of it, to enable SEN children to identify where everything belongs. Asking them to choose and/or tidy away resources will help them to develop independence.

Have some sessions where everyone plays with the maths equipment on the floor. As well as being an effective way of including the child who works at floor level in group activities, this will give the rest of the children an opportunity to develop sensitivity to other people's situations and needs.

> *Early learning goals and the maths area*
> Time spent in the maths area can focus on the following early learning goals:
> - Work as part of a group or class, taking turns and sharing fairly, understanding that there need to be agreed values and codes of behaviour for groups of people, including adults and children, to work together harmoniously.
> - Select and use activities and resources independently.
> - Have a developing awareness of their own needs, views and feelings, and be sensitive to the needs, views and feelings of others.

The book and story corner

Books and stories are valuable aids for:

- boosting the self-image of SEN children through the sharing of literature that deals with SEN in a positive way;
- giving SEN children who may be good at literacy the chance to show off their skills, e.g. through identifying words or reading a sentence;
- encouraging SEN children to contribute to discussions about the story or book and to listen to others' contributions;
- developing the ability of SEN children to concentrate – begin by expecting them to sit for only as long as they are able, and then gradually increase the length of time, praising them in front of others when they manage to maintain attention, even for a short while;
- introducing SEN children to other cultures and beliefs – they may have a limited experience of these because of their difficulties.

> *Handy hints*
> ☞ Use familiar stories and poems to create role-play situations for children with language, social and/or sensory difficulties. The symbolic, imaginative and/or dramatic play of these children may need to be developed, and their involvement in plays and re-enactments will give them support.
>
> ☞ Use puppets to enable the children to explore roles and situations. Because they aren't real and don't make demands, puppets can be a better way of helping SEN children to learn how to be aware of other people's needs and to develop imaginative play.

> *Early learning goals and the book and story corner*
> Time spent in the book and story corner can focus on the following early learning goals:
> - Maintain attention, concentrate, and sit quietly when appropriate.
> - Understand that people have different needs, views, cultures and beliefs, that need to be treated with respect.
> - Understand that they can expect others to treat their needs, views, cultures and beliefs with respect.

The art and craft area

Use art and craft to:

- boost the self-esteem of children with physical problems – who may find difficulty in manipulating the equipment and materials for creative play – by praising their efforts and achievements;
- develop independence by encouraging SEN children to select for themselves the resources needed for their chosen activities, e.g. they find the paints, brushes, water pots, aprons, etc. to paint a picture;
- encourage cooperative activities by challenging pairs or small groups, including SEN children, to work together on an art or craft project, e.g. a model, a frieze or a poster;
- bolster the self-help skills of SEN children by encouraging them to take off their aprons and wash their hands after the art session.

Handy hints

Fill a washing-up bowl with thick paint and encourage an SEN child and a partner to feel each other's fingers in the paint, before asking them to do a joint finger-painting on a large sheet of paper.

Ask an SEN child and partner/group to discuss and decide on a model – if necessary give them two or three ideas to choose from. Let them make their model, ensuring the SEN child is included.

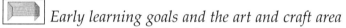 *Early learning goals and the art and craft area*

Time spent in the art and craft area can focus on the following early learning goals:

- Select and use activities and resources independently.
- Dress and undress independently and manage their own personal hygiene.
- Work as part of a group or class, taking turns and sharing fairly, understanding that there need to be agreed values and codes of behaviour for groups of people, including adults and children, to work together harmoniously.

Table-top activities

Using table-top activities, SEN children can:

- develop independence by choosing an activity – at first, give children a choice from only two or three, since they may find it impossible to make a decision when faced with a larger range of activities;
- play in pairs and/or small groups with board or card games – learning rules, turn-taking and waiting patiently are all crucial to personal development and are difficult for some SEN children to grasp;
- learn how to overcome their difficulties when doing an activity, e.g. Lear (1999) suggests giving children with physical difficulties a scrubbing brush to hold their cards or 'beads' made from cardboard tubes for threading activities.

Case study

Noel, aged 6, has ADHD. He is playing a matching game with Carrie and Elizabeth, the Learning Support Assistant (LSA). Noel takes several shapes in his hands.

Elizabeth: Noel, it's Carrie's turn first. Put those back and you can have your go in a minute.

Noel: I want to play.

Elizabeth: Yes, you can, after Carrie. Put the shapes here.

Elizabeth shows Noel where to put back the shapes and he replaces them. Carrie matches two shapes, then looks at Noel.

Carrie: Your turn now.

Elizabeth: Noel – choose a shape. Good boy. Now look for another one that's the same. Yes, that's right. What a clever lad you are!

Noel: My turn now.

Carrie: No, it's my turn, isn't it, Elizabeth?

Elizabeth: Yes. Noel, it's Carrie's turn now and you can have another go in a minute.

Elizabeth catches Noel's attention by touching him gently, making eye contact and using his name before speaking. She breaks the task down into single steps and gives Noel praise for each success. When Noel begins to lose concentration, Elizabeth brings the activity to a close.

Handy hints

☞ Use 'one-player' table-top resources for group activities involving SEN children. For example, make patterns with pegs and pegboards, each child placing a peg in turn once they have agreed as a group what the pattern will be; do a joint jigsaw puzzle by placing a piece in turn; ask children to take it in turns to thread a bead onto the same piece of string, having chosen a pattern beforehand.

☞ Help SEN children to develop responsibility and confidence by appointing them to 'check out' and 'check back in' the resources for a table-top session. They could keep track of items by attaching to a chart a picture of each game or piece of equipment taken out (using Blu-Tack) and then removing it as soon as it is replaced at the end of the session.

Early learning goals and table-top activities
Time spent on table-top activities can focus on the following early learning goals:
- Work as part of a group or class, taking turns and sharing fairly, understanding that there need to be agreed values and codes of behaviour for groups of people, including adults and children, to work together harmoniously.
- Select and use activities and resources independently.
- Consider the consequences of their words and actions for themselves and others.

Small equipment activities

Use small equipment to:

- help hyperactive children to play in pairs/small groups, e.g. with a soft ball and bat, or throwing and catching beanbags – when they show signs of losing interest, finish the game;
- help SEN children to resolve disputes and problems over sharing equipment and so become aware of another person's viewpoint;
- help SEN children to develop symbolic and imaginative play, e.g. using blocks to build a fire-station, play at traffic jams with model cars, etc.

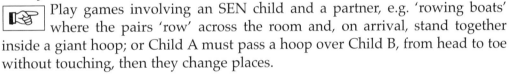

Handy hints

Play games involving an SEN child and a partner, e.g. 'rowing boats' where the pairs 'row' across the room and, on arrival, stand together inside a giant hoop; or Child A must pass a hoop over Child B, from head to toe without touching, then they change places.

Play group games that include SEN children, e.g. the team stands in a line and passes a ball from hand to hand, before an egg timer finishes; or the group sits on the floor in a circle and take it in turns to 'kick' a soft ball to one another.

 Early learning goals and small equipment activities
Time spent on small equipment activities can focus on the following early learning goals:
- Form good relationships with adults and peers.
- Understand what is right, what is wrong and why.
- Consider the consequences of their words and actions for themselves and others.

Large equipment activities

Use a variety of large equipment to:

- help visually impaired children explore their environment and experience cooperative play, e.g. through group play with tricycles, by enabling a child to discover the area available with his peers' support, or through exploring climbing apparatus with other children;

- encourage children with medical conditions such as cystic fibrosis to play actively (e.g. with a buggy, on a swing, or a tricycle), without excessive exertion;
- give physically and/or sensory impaired children new experiences and sensations that they can then be encouraged to talk about, e.g. a partially sighted child on a mini-trampoline;
- help the children with social difficulties to work in pairs/groups/cooperative situations, e.g. on a seesaw or a problem-solving activity such as moving a large block from A to B.

Handy hints

Use chalk lines to mark out a river on the floor or ground and 'infest' it with crocodiles (cardboard tubes). Help the children, including those with SEN, to devise a way of crossing the river without being eaten, using some of the large equipment.

Ask advice from the physiotherapist or occupational therapist on the best way of adapting large equipment to include children with physical difficulties. Often a simple adjustment or addition is enough to enable these children to access equipment.

Early learning goals and large equipment activities

Time spent on large equipment activities can help focus on the following early learning goals:

- Be confident to try new activities, initiate ideas and speak in a familiar group.
- Respond to significant experiences, showing a range of feelings when appropriate.
- Work as part of a group or class, taking turns and sharing fairly, understanding that there need to be agreed values and codes of behaviour for groups of people, including adults and children, to work together harmoniously.

Further reading

Supporting Children with Behaviour Difficulties: A Guide for Assistants in Schools by Glenys Fox (David Fulton Publishers, 2001).
Understanding Children's Challenging Behaviour by Penny Mukherji (Nelson Thornes, 2001).
(Ignore the outdated information on pages 101–3, regarding the SEN Code of Practice.)
Understanding Young Children's Behaviour by J. Rodd (Allen and Unwin, 1996).

3 Communication, language and literacy

> *This chapter covers:*
> - communication, language and literacy and the special needs child
> - communication, language and literacy early learning goals and the special needs child
> - communication, language and literacy in the working areas of the setting

Communication, language and literacy and the special needs child

We must never forget when planning the other 'areas' of our teaching programmes that language (and therefore communication and literacy) permeates every aspect of the curriculum. We should be alert to possible language problems that children face, whether in speech, language, a combination of the two, communication and/or social communication and so on – all difficulties that affect the development of literacy skills. Some children's language difficulties may already have been recognised and they could even be using an alternative communication system such as signing, Makaton or Braille. In this case, try to learn the system and use it. The Special Educational Needs Coordinator (SENCO) or your LEA's Support Service for Sensory Impairment/Special Needs will be able to advise you on how to go about this.

Make sure that SEN children's speaking and listening skills are developing as well as possible before embarking on literacy work. Unless children have some abilities in oral and aural language, they will be unable to make the link between the spoken and heard word and the written and read word – writing will be seen as nothing more than marks on paper. Visual and hearing abilities play a major role in acquiring literacy skills, as does the child's learning ability and, to a certain extent, his physical capabilities. Investigate any apparent problems in these areas.

Communication, language and literacy early learning goals and the special needs child

Communication

Speaking and listening are vital for communication, forming relationships and social interaction, so we must help SEN children to develop their speaking and listening abilities. We should guard against asking the children both too many questions and too many closed questions. Make statements to draw children into a two-way conversation, replacing the likes of 'Do you help Grandpa in the garden?' with 'When

I was a little girl, I used to help my Grandpa grow all sorts of flowers and vegetables in his garden.' This will probably result in the child offering much more than the 'Yes' or 'No' answer to the first question.

Be aware of tone of voice, intonation, gesture and non-verbal language. Children with hearing problems may be unable to differentiate between voice tones, while those with autistic spectrum disorders find extreme difficulty in interpreting non-verbal communication. Children with severe cerebral palsy who are in constant spasm will have great difficulty in making controlled physical gestures that are part of non-verbal communication.

Language

Some SEN children have problems with the social and personal aspects that are integral to language. Children with autistic spectrum disorders, for example, interpret language literally, so if you say 'I'm only pulling your leg', they will wonder what you mean because you haven't even touched their leg. These subtleties of language may also be very difficult for children with sensory impairments since they have been deprived of the visual or aural stimuli that are all part of the complexities of language. Children with physical difficulties face similar problems as a result of their limited physical and sensory experiences. They may not know what it feels like, for example, to run fast or to jump off apparatus, so all the resulting vocabulary from these activities will be theoretical.

Literacy

It is a quantum leap from the spoken to the written word, which we take for granted because we are literate. For many SEN children that leap is a chasm that will take time and lots of support to jump across. The abstract nature of literacy (spoken and written words can't be measured and weighed, nor are they consistent in form) makes it a very difficult concept for SEN children, so their need for plenty of concrete and practical experience has to be planned for even more carefully.

Make available alternative literacy systems such as Braille or audio books, exploit technology and use the multi-sensory computer software that is available. Use activities such as rhymes and jingles, particularly action rhymes, since this helps children to develop sequential memory, to see patterns and repetitions, to predict, to hear 'rhyming families' and so on – all crucial skills for the development of literacy. Share a wide variety of books so that children see that writing and reading have many different purposes beyond 'just' stories. Encourage them to explore books alone so that sometimes they see the printed word on their own terms and in their own time.

Communication, language and literacy in the working areas of the setting

The home corner

Turn the home corner into:

- a picnic area for a floor level activity: help the children to write and send invitations to join the picnic; list who is coming and what they will eat; make the picnic food, pack and label the lunch boxes; go to the picnic area on a bus (with seats on the floor); distribute each child's lunch by reading the labels; eat the picnic; tidy up and take home all the litter; catch the bus home;

- a bus for a (wheel)chair level activity: help the children to decide on roles; design and make tickets, adverts and signs for the inside of the bus; collect or make the money; choose a destination; arrange the bus's layout; go on the journey; discuss the scenery en route; reach the terminus;
- a hospital with the beds at floor level: help the children to make the patients' charts, X-rays, prescriptions and so on; decide on roles; lay out the hospital ward; have examinations, operations and other surgical procedures such as administering medication; take some X-rays; apply bandages and plasters; have a visitors' time; discharge the patients.

Handy hints

☞ Use puppets or masks to engage children whose SEN makes them reluctant or unable to interact with other people. Such children sometimes find it easier to become involved because the puppets aren't real people and don't appear to make the same social and intellectual demands. (See Photocopiable Sheets 3 and 4 on pages 39 and 40.)

☞ Get children to lie on paper on the floor and draw around them. Use differently textured materials to 'dress' the figures, such as fake fur for the hair, rubber for wellies, fleece for a jumper and so on. This gives tactile experiences to children with visual impairment or autistic spectrum disorders.

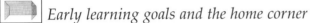 *Early learning goals and the home corner*

Time spent in the home corner can focus on the following early learning goals:

- Interact with others, negotiating plans and activities and taking turns in conversations.
- Enjoy listening to and using spoken and written language, and readily turn to it in their play and learning.
- Use language to imagine and recreate roles and experiences.
- Use talk to organise, sequence, and clarify thinking, ideas, feelings and events.
- Attempt writing for various purposes, using features of different forms such as lists, stories and instructions.

Sand and water play

Use the sand and water play to:

- explore sensory experiences: 'What does the sand feel like?', 'Blow through the straw into the water – what does it sound like?', 'What did you smell when I added this to the water?', 'What did you feel after I added the warm water?', 'Dribble this colour slowly into the water – what's happened?', 'Drag your fingers through this (dry/wet) sand – what does it feel like?', 'Bang the bottom of the water tray – what does it sound like?'
- help the children to generalise a new language concept, e.g. if they have learnt 'too much', 'spill' and 'pour' in the water play, get them to pour the morning milk into the mugs, giving them the chance to use the same vocabulary in a different context;

- bring in literacy skills, e.g. if the children have been playing with different containers and their quantities, help them to record this with either a caption or a word; encourage them to read their writing at different times throughout the day.

Case study

Jamie, aged 5, has dyspraxia and his IEP is targeting his gross and fine motor skills. He is playing with wet sand to help his coordination, hand and finger awareness, muscle strength, and tone and dexterity. Susan, the LSA, works with him. She encourages him to use the spade to fill the containers with sand.

Jamie: It's hard, the sand's hard to do.

Susan: Because there's water in it, it's hard – it makes it difficult.

Jamie: Yeh – s'difficult. Number work's difficult too.

Susan: No. You're good at number work – it's not difficult.

Jamie: No, my number work's not difficult, but Saul's is. It's difficult for him.

Susan: What's the first sound in 'difficult'?

Jamie: 'D'. Like in 'David'.

Jamie experiments with the word 'difficult', applying it to himself in the sand play situation and also to another area of his work. When challenged by Susan he then goes on to use the word in relation to his brother. Susan takes the opportunity to slip in a quick literacy question while she has Jamie's interest.

Handy hints

Freeze water in a container. Let visually impaired children have a fun sensory experience, handling ice at different stages of thawing and experimenting with different toys and the ice. (Make sure little hands don't become too cold!) How many words can they discover to describe the ice?

Bury small objects in soft, dry sand and have a Treasure Hunt. The children search and find an object and then have to describe it in the language terms they are working on, e.g. colour, size, shape, etc. Make this into a game that can be played by an individual or small group of children, as required, when working on a socialising/interacting IEP.

 Early learning goals and sand and water play

Time spent in sand and water play can focus on the following early learning goals:

- Interact with others, negotiating plans and activities and taking turns in conversations.
- Sustain attentive listening, responding to what they have heard by relevant comments, questions and actions.
- Extend their vocabulary, exploring the meanings and sounds of new words.

The music corner

Use the music corner to:

- enable groups, including SEN children, to compose a piece of music: record their music on paper, allocating a different letter to a picture of each instrument (e.g. 't' for tambourine, 'd' for drum and so on), then show the letters and pictures in the sequence of playing. If several instruments play simultaneously, write the symbols vertically (see Figures 3.1 and 3.2);
- expose the children to music vocabulary, e.g. 'loud(er)', 'bang', 'blow', 'quiet(er)', 'tap', 'shake', etc.;
- help SEN children who have difficulty in retaining instructions by gradually building them up:
  1. ask the child to shake the bell
  2. ask the child to shake the bell after Joe bangs the drum
  3. ask him to shake it quietly, after Joe bangs the drum
  4. ask him to shake it quietly twice, after Joe bangs the drum
- give the child practice in sequencing, rhythm and patterns, all of which are crucial to the development of literacy skills.

Handy hints

Use different-sized drums, played with varying degrees of force, and let the hearing impaired children enjoy a sensory experience. Take turns to play the instrument so they can learn how to hit the drums with hard or light strikes, as well as feel the resulting vibrations. Have fun thinking of words to describe the different sensations they experience from the different quality vibrations.

Press-gang the science coordinator or a willing parent to rig up a circuit using batteries and light bulbs connected to musical instruments. When the instruments are played by children with hearing impairment, the light goes on, giving them feedback.

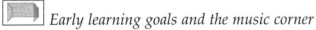 *Early learning goals and the music corner*

Time spent in the music corner can focus on the following early learning goals:

- Interact with others, negotiating plans and activities and taking turns in conversation.
- Sustain attentive listening, responding to what they have heard by relevant comments, questions and actions.
- Listen with enjoyment, and respond to stories, songs and other music, rhymes and poems and make up their own stories, songs, rhymes and poems.

The maths area

In the maths area SEN children can:

- use the 'practical' maths equipment in play situations, e.g. experiment with the scales, explore ways of measuring their height, etc.;

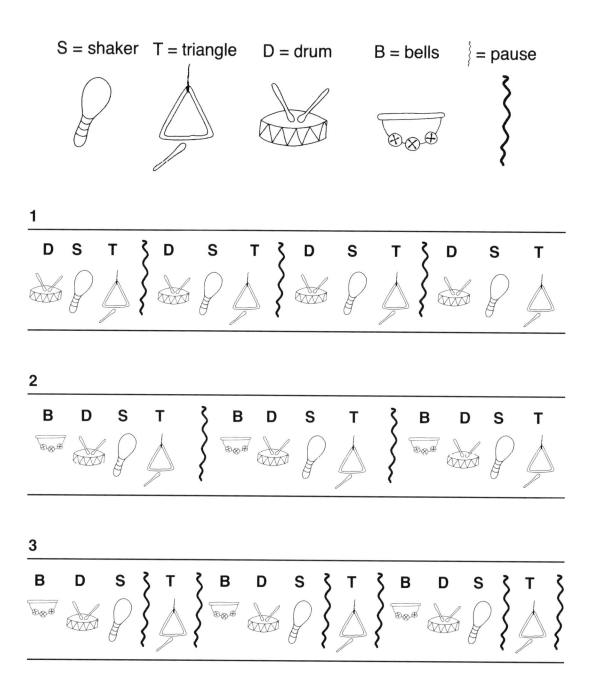

Figure 3.1 Examples of simple musical notation for consecutive playing

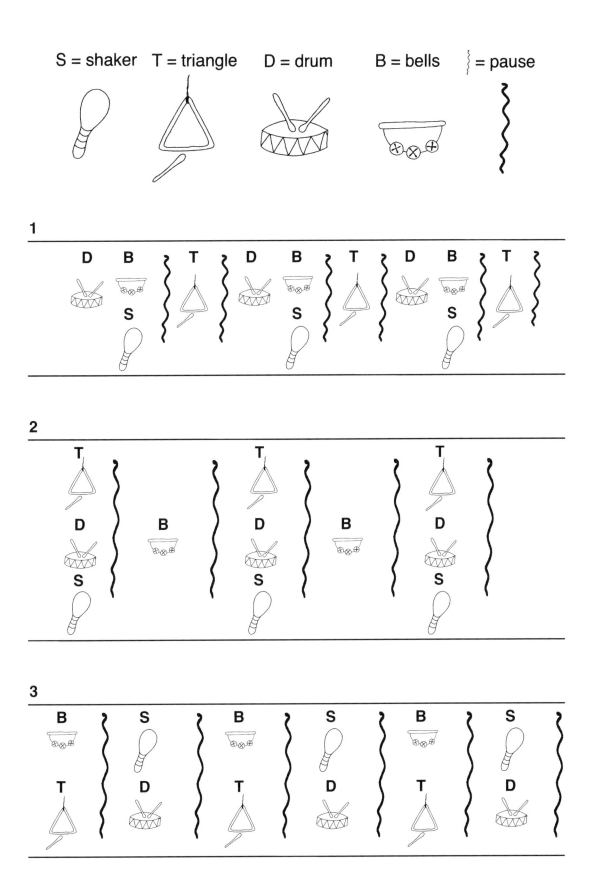

Figure 3.2 Examples of simple musical notation for simultaneous playing

- play in groups to develop their interaction skills, e.g. start off with only you and a single child, before inviting another child to join you, and gradually increase the size of the group as the child's confidence in this situation grows;
- enjoy discovering number concepts, starting with their own direct experiences and concrete examples, e.g. if a child is working on 'two', he may have two sisters, two dogs or two gloves to start with; help him to draw and label everything that he has two of; encourage him to collect, classify, name and label in sets of two, objects from around the room; reinforce numbers by playing with all the small maths equipment;
- be encouraged to reapply new maths concepts in different contexts, e.g. they can be given lots of practical and concrete experience in each situation and then helped to generalise it.

Handy hints

☞ When working on a specific number, play 'I spy' with SEN children, to find the number in the room: the clock, dominoes, dice, the computer keyboard, wall charts or captions, number tracks, the shop till and height charts are all possible sources.

☞ Record onto a cassette, instructions that are written on a task card, and leave them out for the children to explore independently. If, for example, they are working on shape, record instructions such as 'Find a (red) circle', 'Find a (blue) square' onto the cassette, as appropriate. Leave enough space between each instruction to allow the tape recorder to be switched off and on again without losing the voice. On the task card, draw and label the relevant shapes for the children to match.

▦ *Early learning goals and the maths area*

Time spent in the maths area can focus on the following early learning goals:
- Interact with others, negotiating plans and activities and taking turns in conversations.
- Use talk to organise, sequence, and clarify thinking, ideas, feelings and events.
- Attempt writing for various purposes, using features of different forms such as lists, stories and instructions.

The book and story corner

Use a storybook to:

- explore sequences, using vocabulary such as 'beginning', 'next', 'then', 'afterwards', 'end' and so on; some SEN children are able to retain only the most recent event in the story;
- help the child to predict the next part, having paused partway through a story; many SEN children find this extremely difficult and they need lots of practice;
- help the children to make inferences from a story, e.g. if the main character is crying ask the children why, helping them to explore all possible reasons;

- make opportunities for the child to write, e.g. words, captions or labels for pictures arising from the story;
- encourage the children to act out the story then ask those with SEN what they will act next, or what the character might say now, etc.

Use non-fiction to:

- expand children's vocabularies; if they have physical or sensory difficulties, their vocabularies may have gaps, so wherever possible give them the physical experiences that reinforce the new vocabulary;
- predict what comes next, e.g. when sharing a book about building a house, ask the child to guess the subsequent stage of the work;
- experiment, through play, with ideas explored in the text, e.g. continuing with the book about house-building, let them build a house with construction toys; encourage them to use the book as their 'action plan'.

Use poetry to:

- help the child to discover the rhythms and rhymes of language, and language patterns;
- memorise sequences;
- predict the next verse or part, particularly in counting rhymes or rhymes with a chorus or regular pattern.

Handy hints

☞ Extend a familiar story beyond its ending. Help the children to make up more adventures for the main character. SEN children may find this difficult, because their language and/or imaginative ability may be limited.

☞ Use non-fiction to practise and reinforce sequencing. Recipes, for example, must be followed in the required order, as should instructions for games.

☞ Have fun with action rhymes and poems. Use musical instruments for an added dimension. Ensure that children with physical and/or sensory difficulties are included.

Early learning goals and the book and story corner

Time spent in the book and story corner can focus on the following early learning goals:
- Use language to imagine and recreate roles and experiences.
- Listen with enjoyment, and respond to stories, songs and other music, rhymes and poems and make up their own stories, songs, rhymes and poems.
- Retell narratives in the correct sequence, drawing on language patterns of stories.
- Show an understanding of the elements of stories, such as main character, sequence of events, and openings, and how information can be found in non-fiction texts to answer questions about where, who, why and how.

The art and craft area

During art and craft activities:

- make sure children know the names of the tools they are using: brush, easel, pot, paint, apron, clay, dough, glue, scissors, etc.;
- help them to learn the vocabulary of *what* they are doing: cutting, drawing, painting, sticking, splashing, rubbing, glueing, etc.;
- expand their vocabulary by talking about *how* they are doing things: cutting carefully, squeezing hard, stirring slowly, etc.;
- explore colour and texture in a wider sense: 'What other colours can the sky be?', 'Let's paint Jack's jumper in a different colour to show he's happy', 'Are leaves always green?', 'Why do you think the paint feels gritty?' 'Let's make it thinner – how?'
- use clay, dough, Plasticine and so on to talk about consistency and weight: 'Yours is harder than mine – can you think why?', 'Let's add some water – what's happened?', 'Why do you think you can't roll that one into a sausage?', 'Is this clay heavier than the dough?'
- exploit cutting and sticking to reinforce concepts as appropriate: 'Let's cut out lots of (red/blue etc.) circles (squares/triangles etc.) and make a pattern. Cut out three of these shapes and two of those. Squeeze the scissors gently as you cut';
- stimulate discussion while model-making: 'How high will it be?', 'What's this bit for?', 'Where will you put the smaller box?', 'What can we use to make it secure?', 'How will that bit work?', 'What can you use for wheels?'

Case study

Rebecca, who is 4 and has mild cerebral palsy, is doing some finger-painting. Lisa, the LSA, has thickened the paints with flour. As Rebecca works, she talks to Lisa about what she is doing.

Rebecca: This isn't runny paint, is it, Lisa? It's runny paint in the other pots.

Lisa: No, this isn't runny paint, it's much thicker. Do you know why?

Rebecca: Because you mixed that stuff in it. Is that stuff glue? The paint's …

Lisa: What?

Rebecca: Sticky.

Lisa: (Laughs) No, it isn't glue, Rebecca, it's flour like we made cakes with yesterday.

Rebecca: Flour? It's flour paint.

Lisa: And the flour's made the paint – what?

Rebecca: Thick.

Lisa: Yes, that's right. Thicker than the other paint.

Rebecca was aware that her paint was different from the other 'runny' paint. She used her experience of glue to try to characterise the consistency of the paint ('sticky'), and then checked by repeating the word 'flour'. Lisa used the opportunity to consolidate Rebecca's vocabulary and widen her experience of the uses of flour.

Handy hints

☞ Use media in different ways to include SEN children, e.g. use scented drawer-lining paper for visually impaired children to make collages with, or do some free style feet-painting with children who have physical difficulties.

☞ Mix thicker paint and put it into old washing-up liquid bottles, to be squeezed out by children who cannot hold and/or control a brush, who need to work on muscle tone in their hands, who don't work at an easel or who have coordination problems.

Early learning goals and the art and craft area
Time spent in the art and craft area can focus on the following early learning goals:
- Enjoy listening to and using spoken and written language, and readily turn to it in their play and learning.
- Sustain attentive listening, respond to what they have heard by relevant comments, questions or actions.
- Use talk to organise, sequence, and clarify thinking, ideas, feelings and events.

Table-top activities

Use table-top activities to:

- reinforce verbs, prepositions and adjectives such as thread, shake, move, tie, hold, through, beside, under, over, next to, along, small, big, soft and quiet;
- reinforce concepts such as colour, size and shape, e.g. 'What pattern will you make with the beads?', 'How about making a pattern based on size – big/little/big/little?'
- foster cooperative play, e.g. by playing a group board game, or jointly completing a jigsaw; these involve the children in turn-taking and logical thinking;
- do activities such as bead-threading, Jack straws, board games, jigsaws, form boards and so on to practise logical thinking, predicting, sequencing, pattern-making, etc.

Handy hints

☞ Practise sequencing by asking the children to help you to write the instructions for their favourite board games. Let them dictate while you scribe. Have fun trying to play the game if their instructions are wrong – can they correct their original attempt?

☞ Practise logical thinking by playing very simple 'Riddles' using picture cards, e.g. 'This is an animal with four legs and it barks.' If three elements are too many, reduce it to 'It's got four legs and it barks' or even to 'It barks.'

Early learning goals and table-top activities
Time spent on table-top activities can focus on the following early learning goals:
- Interact with others, negotiating plans and activities and taking turns in conversations.
- Use talk to organise, sequence, and clarify thinking, ideas, feelings and events.
- Attempt writing for different purposes, using features of different forms such as lists, stories and instructions.

Small equipment activities

Use the small equipment for:

- conversation skills, e.g. 'Shall we use a soft ball for this game? Why?', 'Let's invent a game with the beanbags and the bucket – how will it work?'
- literacy activities such as labelling and listing the equipment and storage boxes, writing and reading instructions, etc.;
- practising prediction – 'What will happen if I throw the quoit at the skittle?'

Handy hints
 If children have difficulty catching, let them use a bucket or washing-up bowl initially rather than their hands, as this will widen the 'landing area'.

 Helping children to list the equipment needed for particular activities will not only help them to develop organisational and sequencing skills, but will also give practice in writing and, later, reading the lists.

 Early learning goals and small equipment activities
Time spent on small equipment activities can focus on the following early learning goals:
- Enjoy listening to and using spoken and written language, and readily turn to it in their play and learning.
- Use talk to organise, sequence, and clarify thinking, ideas, feelings and events.
- Attempt writing for different purposes, using features of different forms such as lists, stories and instructions.

Large equipment activities

Use the large equipment to:

- work on language that the children can apply to themselves through their actions: climb, jump, run, slide, crawl, fast, high, spin and so on;
- reinforce and generalise prepositions such as through, under, over, in, on, etc.;

- encourage the children to tell you how it feels when they play with different pieces of equipment, e.g. the sensation of being on the swing or crawling through the tunnel;
- explore comparatives such as high and higher, fast and faster, long and longer, etc.;
- introduce superlatives such as highest, fastest and longest;
- help the child with social and/or language difficulties through cooperative play, e.g. one child waits for the other at the end of the slide before they both crawl through the tunnel, or two (or more) children use tricycles and trailers together to 'deliver' milk, papers and letters to houses.

Handy hints

Label each piece of equipment with the appropriate action word, such as 'climb', 'ride' or 'jump' and an accompanying picture. Talk about it together for a moment or two, exploring the word and picture as the children choose their activities.

Hide differently textured or scented materials on large equipment to give sensory impaired children (and the others!) a surprise. For example, attach a piece of fur fabric to the handrail at the top of the slide or put some scented cloth on the roof in the centre of the tunnel.

Early learning goals and large equipment activities
Time spent on large equipment activities can focus on the following early learning goals:
- Interact with others, negotiating plans and activities and taking turns in conversations.
- Enjoy listening to and using spoken and written language, and readily turn to it in their play and learning.
- Use talk to organise, sequence, and clarify thinking, ideas, feelings and events.

Further reading

Autism in the Early Years by Val Cumine, Julia Leach and Gill Stevenson (David Fulton Publishers, 2000).
Spoken Language Difficulties: Practical Strategies and Activities for Teachers and Other Professionals by Lynn Stuart, Felicity Wright, Sue Grigor and Alison Howey (David Fulton Publishers, 2002).
Children's Minds by Margaret Donaldson (Fontana, 1978).

Useful addresses

Association For All Speech Impaired Children (AFASIC)
50–52 Great Sutton Street
London EC1V 0DJ
Tel: 020 7490 9410 (admin.)
Helpline: 0845 3555577
Fax: 020 7251 2834

I CAN
4 Dyers Building
Holborn
London EC1N 2QP
Tel: 08700 104066
Fax: 08700 104067
website: www.ican.org.uk

National Autistic Society
393 City Road
London EC1V 1NE
Helpline: 0870 6008585
Tel: 020 7833 2299
Fax: 020 7833 9666
email: nas@nasorg.uk

Photocopiable Sheet 3

Use this sheet as a template to make a mask with the child. You can vary the features according to the child's design.

Photocopiable Sheet 4

Use this sheet to make finger puppets to play with. Let the child choose the features.

4 Mathematical development

This chapter covers:
- maths and the special needs child
- the maths early learning goals and the special needs child
- mathematical development in the working areas of the setting

Maths and the special needs child

Mathematics is involved in almost every aspect of daily living, with a huge vocabulary that is shared with other areas of learning. Children should be helped to enjoy maths and have fun learning and experimenting with mathematical concepts by playing with equipment, games and resources. By using the resources in the setting in a fun way, children become familiar with the everyday application of number, shape, space, time and measurement, and with the language that is an integral part of these concepts.

Children with SEN may take longer to understand mathematical concepts than their peers, but we should still provide every opportunity possible for them to explore, experiment and enjoy learning about maths. It is important to understand that while children may enter the early years setting with apparent mathematical knowledge and abilities, we cannot always be certain that 'what you see is what you get'. For example, a child may be able to count by rote to five, or even to ten, with confidence, but when asked to demonstrate his understanding of the concept of 'three', he may be completely stuck – counting by rote does not prove that a concept of number has been consolidated.

Be prepared to give SEN children lots of opportunities for repetition and revision of mathematical concepts. Abstract ideas can be very difficult for them to grasp and they need as many concrete examples as possible to help them to develop their mathematical skills.

The maths early learning goals and the special needs child

Number

Every day we use numbers almost without realising it: page numbers, clock faces, radio stations, bus numbers, timetables, prices – the list is endless. Children learn numbers' names and symbols through daily contact with television channels, buses and cars, shop signs, school notices and so on, and they learn that we use numbers to count in a systematic way. They then need to develop a concept of the 'numberness' of numbers, one-to-one correspondence, and the stability of numbers. Young children learn how to count by rote fairly early on by experiencing the constant repetition of the order of numbers in the songs, rhymes, games and counting jingles that they are exposed to almost from birth. Children with learning difficulties may have the ability to 'count' to a certain point, but remember that this skill is often quite simply that – the ability to repeat a sequence of numbers in the correct order. While this is a valuable skill, which later assists in many other areas of the curriculum, it must not be taken as a sign that the child 'knows' numbers. An interesting check is to ask the child to start counting from a later number, e.g. five. Does he continue with 'six, seven, eight'? Does he say, 'five, one, two, three'? Does he just look blank and say nothing? His reaction will reveal whether or not he understands that numbers continue in a specific order.

Number can be a very difficult concept for children with special needs. Help them by devising lots of fun and interesting activities using equipment and apparatus that physically demonstrate the point being made. They also need lots of experience relating numbers to their everyday experiences, making abstract concepts more concrete and real for them. Exploit opportunities that crop up during free play, to point out anything that relates to the number concept they are working on.

Shape

Children should have the experience of exploring and learning about the properties and characteristics of shapes, both two- and three-dimensional. SEN children may need a little more help to discover what makes a circle a circle or a cube a cube, but with familiarity, repetition and lots of practical experience, they will assimilate the characteristics of each one. From the specific examples explored within the setting, children then need to be encouraged to apply what they have learnt to the world around them, e.g. they can identify the wheels on a car as being circles, or a mirror on the bathroom wall as a square.

Space

Space and shape are closely linked. A child's spatial awareness, both of himself in his environment and of the objects around him, is a crucial part of his development. This is an area that can often be problematical for SEN children. Encourage and help them to explore with 3D shapes to build models, create a situation for imaginary play such as using large blocks to make a bus, or see if and how they can fit different 3D shapes together.

Two-dimensional shapes and the relationship between them are also very important concepts that need to be acquired. A circle, for example, cannot fit exactly into a square, but two triangles might be able to. Use the shapes to create abstract pictures or patterns and the child will discover that some shapes can be tessellated whereas others cannot.

Measures

The concept of measurement will be acquired by children through the games and activities that they experience in the daily routines of the setting. Sand and water play using different containers helps to put across the ideas of more, less, full, empty, the same, big, little and so on. Opportunities can arise in the home corner, on the large play equipment or in art for discussing quantities and making comparisons between sizes and amounts. Use each chance as it occurs to help children to see, do and understand the concept of measurement.

Mathematical development in the working areas of the setting

The home corner

Use the home corner for:

- number concepts: turn the area into a café and have menus, the 'food' itself and all the accompanying labels; play maths in the café: 'I'd like two of the round cakes and three square biscuits please', 'One large cup of tea and two small cups of coffee', 'Put fewer beans on my baby's plate please', 'I'd like my juice in a tall glass', 'How many pennies do you need?', 'How many scones are left?', 'Make sure everyone has a cup and saucer' (one-to-one correspondence), 'Could we have two more ice-creams please?'
- dressing up to stimulate maths discussions: 'I can't put that dress on because I'm too tall', 'That's not long enough for you, Gemma, you're shorter than David, so this cloak will fit you, The one he has is too long for you', 'That skirt is wider than this one – which one do you think will fit me?', 'How many dresses do we have to choose from?', 'There were five hats in here and John, Ahmed and Justin have all got one, How many are there left in the box?'

Handy hints

When introducing a new maths concept to SEN children through the home corner, begin with a situation they have already experienced, i.e. they may not yet have visited a café. A new situation can be introduced later when they have consolidated the concept.

Children with autistic spectrum disorders are often very good at maths. Use this to work on their social and interaction skills in the home corner by involving them in group play.

 Early learning goals and the home corner

Time spent in the home corner can focus on the following early learning goals:
- Say and use number names in order in familiar contexts.
- Use language such as 'more' or 'less' to compare two numbers.
- Use everyday words to describe position.
- Use developing mathematical ideas and methods to solve everyday problems.

Sand and water play

Use sand and water play to:

- explore mathematical concepts such as light and heavy or more and less, e.g. use both wet and dry sand to explore these;
- play with the children and use mathematical language to help them to understand it and use it appropriately: 'Shall we see whether this box needs more than that one?', 'Do you think we can fill this one to the top? Why not?', 'Which one has less sand in it?', 'Why do you think the wet sand won't go back in?, Is it heavier than the dry sand?, Why do you think that is?'

- explore concepts such as more, less, big, small, heavy and light, using toys, the sand or water trays (different-sized containers, spoons and diggers): 'Does the water-wheel spin faster with more water or less water?, How do we make it go slower?', 'What happens when we pour the water from the big jug into the small one?'

Handy hints

 Help children with visual problems by colouring the water or scenting it, and by making the sand have different consistencies by adding more or less water. Talk about the way that 'more' or 'less' water affects the sand.

Make up sets of familiar objects according to the number being worked on, e.g. two apples, dolls, spoons, clocks, socks, etc. and leave them in a table display for the children to explore in their own time.

Early learning goals and sand and water play

Time spent in sand and water play can focus on the following early learning goals:
- Use developing mathematical ideas and methods to solve practical problems.
- Use language such as 'greater', 'smaller', 'heavier', or 'lighter' to compare quantities.
- Use everyday words to describe position.

The music corner

Use music for:

- singing counting songs such as 'One, two, three, four, five, once I caught a fish alive', 'Ten fat sausages', 'Five little ducks', 'Ten green bottles', 'Five currant buns' – SEN children need to reinforce number sequences; the songs also introduce subtraction and addition through the use of counting back or counting on sequences;
- encouraging the children to physically act numbers, by role-playing the parts, (the sausages, the bottles, the currant buns, etc.) or by holding up models of the items in the songs – again, concrete examples of a concept;
- looking at, talking about and playing the instruments so that children can use mathematical language and develop mathematical concepts: 'Are the handles long or short?', 'Is the drum heavy?', 'What shape is it?', 'Who can play a triangle?', 'How many sides does it have?', 'Is it the same shape as the drum?', 'How many bars are there on the xylophone?', 'Which one is the longest?', 'How many instruments are there in our band?', 'Are there more shakers or more bangers?', 'Is the shaker full or empty?', 'Is the xylophone longer than the drumstick?'

Case study
Bethan, aged 5, is partially sighted and is playing freely in the music corner with Adrian. She shakes a tin containing dried peas, while Adrian plays with a larger tin also filled with peas.

Bethan: Play yours and I'll play mine.

Adrian: Mine's bigger.

(They play the tins together and then separately)

Bethan: They sound different 'cos yours is bigger.

Adrian: I bet mine's got a million thousand peas in.

Bethan is aware that the size of the tins affects their sound; both children use the term 'bigger'; Adrian uses a numerical term ('a million thousand') showing his awareness of a large quantity.

Handy hints

Help the children to compose their own music, and bring in maths while they work. Encourage the children to record their music on paper, e.g. if three triangles, two shakers and a drum play together, they draw the appropriate number of shapes in a column on the paper; if the instruments are played successively, they draw the shapes in a line (see Figures 3.1 and 3.2, on pages 30 and 31).

Help children with sensory and/or physical difficulties to make their own musical instruments. Use empty boxes filled with different contents such as pebbles or lentils to give different sounds, empty tins again with different fillings, tubes, washing-up liquid bottles and so on. Discuss the shapes, weights, sounds, capacity, etc. of each instrument.

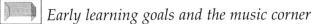 *Early learning goals and the music corner*

Time spent in the music corner can focus on the following early learning goals:
- Say and use number names in familiar contexts.
- Use developing mathematical ideas and methods to solve practical problems.
- Begin to relate addition to combining two groups of objects and subtraction to 'taking away'.

The maths area

Use the maths area to:

- explore numbers: play with bricks, small toys, beads, counters, buttons, number lines, sorting sets and so on; give lots of practice and encouragement, and don't move on until each number has been grasped;

- present numerals and two- and three-dimensional shapes in different textures (e.g. felt, sandpaper, rubber, etc.) so children with sensory impairment can feel them;
- explore shapes by sorting and matching; be careful not to overload children with too many at the same time – those with learning difficulties may take a long time to assimilate each shape's characteristics so be prepared to let them explore at length;
- experiment with weight using familiar objects in the scales; don't introduce standardised weights since SEN children should consolidate the concepts of heavier and lighter first;
- explore length and height using familiar objects including the children themselves! Avoid standardised units since they need to grasp concepts such as long, short, high, tall, wide and so on.

Handy hints

☞ When measuring the children's heights, get them to lie on the floor so that SEN children who work at floor level can be included. Children in a wheelchair can be included if you use string to measure all the children as they sit in their chairs, then compare the lengths of string.

☞ Let visually impaired children use 2D shapes to make patterns. For an extra dimension, make the shapes from differently textured materials to give a tactile experience.

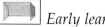 *Early learning goals and the maths area*

Time spent in the maths area can focus on the following early learning goals:
- Say and use number names in familiar contexts.
- Use language such as 'greater', 'smaller', 'heavier' or 'lighter' to compare quantities.
- Use language such as 'circle' or 'bigger' to describe the shape and size of solids and flat shapes.

The book and story corner

In the book and story corner:

- use traditional stories such as *Snow White* or *Goldilocks* to reinforce mathematical concepts, e.g. counting, one-to-one correspondence (a bed per dwarf or a bowl per bear), big, small/little, high, low, tall, short and so on;
- use classics such as *The Very Hungry Caterpillar* by Eric Carle (Hamish Hamilton 1969) to count, to discuss the size and shape of the fruits and vegetables, to discuss the length of the caterpillar, etc.;
- use poetry and traditional rhymes to have fun with number e.g. *Nonsense Counting Rhymes* by Kaye Umansky (OUP 1999) for practice in counting forwards or backwards;
- see how the page numbers in all books follow the same sequence.

Handy hints

☞ Help the children to make models of things from counting poems and nursery rhymes, e.g. Five currant buns or This old man (drum, shoe, tree), and use the models to count, weigh, measure and so on. Children with learning difficulties will benefit from these concrete examples.

☞ Make number boxes with a textured numeral on each (for the visually impaired) – shoeboxes are a good size for this. Play different games: ask children to fill them with the correct number of small toys; put in too many and invite children to correct it; put in too few and ask them to make up the right amount; instruct the children to put circles/squares/rectangles and other shapes in the box, and so on.

▦ *Early learning goals and the book and story corner*

Time spent in the book and story corner can focus on the following early learning goals:
- Count reliably up to ten everyday objects.
- Recognise numerals 1 to 9.
- Use everyday words to describe position.

The art and craft area

Use art and craft for:

- exploring solid shapes by making junk models; be careful to avoid plastics, polystyrene or empty containers, which may have small traces of allergens, when working with children who have allergies;
- reinforcing flat shapes by using textured materials to make pictures, e.g. corrugated paper, textured wallpaper, etc.;
- exploring weight using different malleable materials;
- using maths to stimulate art, e.g. to make abstract pictures, collages or friezes based on shapes, colours, sizes or quantities;
- reinforcing capacity when filling pots with paint, containers with water and so on – use terms such as 'full', 'empty', 'more' and 'less', involving the child in the preparations;
- exploring measures, e.g. compare paintbrushes with crayons ('longer', 'shorter') or choose the right boxes for a model ('You need a longer one here') etc.

Handy hints

☞ Mark 2D shapes with a 'starting/finishing point' for visually impaired children, e.g. in one corner of a square, triangle or rectangle. When they feel the shape they will be able to count the number of sides and edges from start to finish.

☞ Use malleable materials to make different shapes – either flat or solid – with children who have dyspraxia or other problems with motor skills. As they work, they will be squeezing, rolling, pinching and so on, thus exercising their hand muscles, as well as reinforcing the maths concept.

> *Early learning goals and the art and craft area*
> Time spent in the art and craft area can focus on the following early learning goals:
> - Talk about, recognise and recreate simple patterns.
> - Use language such as 'circle' or 'bigger' to describe the shape and size of solid and flat shapes.
> - Use developing mathematical ideas and methods to solve practical problems.

Table-top activities

Maths is involved when children:

- count the number of spots on the face of dice or on dominoes;
- play board games and count aloud as they move their counters along the spaces;
- match and sort shapes, talking about their size, their colours, their properties and how many there are in each set;
- play card games in a group, using mathematical expressions such as 'the same as', 'more', 'fewer', 'share', 'each', etc.;
- play with blocks or bricks, using terms such as 'heavy', 'light', 'heavier than', 'lighter than', 'big(ger)', 'small(er)', 'more', 'fewer', 'tall', 'short' and 'high';
- make patterns with beads, counters, bricks, etc.;
- share out items among a group, checking whether there are enough, there will be any left over, more are needed, everyone has an equal share and so on;
- compare the different lengths of Jack straws or threading laces.

> *Handy hints*
> When children with motor difficulties or those who work on a tray want to make patterns with small objects, put a dycem mat on the surface to keep the objects secure. Alternatively, use felt shapes, colours and so on.
>
> If children with learning difficulties are working on numbers below seven, make a die with only a 'known' number of dots on each face. If the children know up to 'four', for example, don't draw any more than four dots per face. Use the new die for board games (see Photocopiable Sheet 1 on page 12).

> *Early learning goals and table-top activities*
> Time spent on table-top activities can focus on the following early learning goals:
> - Say and use number names in order in familiar contexts.
> - Talk about, recognise and recreate simple patterns.
> - Recognise numerals 1 to 9.

Small equipment activities

Encourage the children to:

- pick out the shapes on the play mats that have pictures, maps, etc. printed on them;
- measure the distance they throw a ball in terms of longer, higher and so on; get them to compare skipping-ropes or bats of different lengths;
- decide on appropriate solid shapes to complete a model;
- count the different pieces of equipment, e.g. 'How many beanbags are there?', 'How many red balls are there?'

Handy hints

☞ Use small equipment to introduce children with learning difficulties to count abstract things such as throws or catches – the use of physical equipment will help them to make the connection. Record their scores in picture form alongside the numerals.

☞ Ask children with emotional or behavioural difficulties to take responsibility for some of the small equipment by, for example, counting the bats and balls at the beginning and end of a session to check none is missing, or practising one-to-one correspondence by allocating a piece of equipment per child.

Early learning goals and small equipment activities

Time spent on small equipment activities can focus on the following early learning goals:

- Use developing mathematical ideas and methods to solve practical problems.
- Use language such as 'circle' or 'bigger' to describe the shape and size of solid and flat shapes.
- Use everyday words to describe position.

Large equipment activities

Maths is involved when the children:

- talk about size, colour, shape and quantity while they have fun playing on the equipment;
- play in the ball pool and explore concepts such as more, fewer, enough, too many, heavy, light, long(er), short(er), etc.;
- play on the climbing frame and talk about tall, short, high and low; how many ropes there are, whether they are long or short, how many bars there are, whether more children can fit on, what shape the tyre-swings are;
- talk about how many wheels a tricycle has, how many a bicycle has, how many a trailer or cart has, how many pedals there are, what shape the wheels and the pedals are, what colour each piece of equipment is, whether there are more bikes or more prams, whether the buggy is taller than the pram or the trailer is longer than the tricycle, if the swing goes higher than the seesaw, if the slide is taller than the climbing frame, how many steps it has, if the tunnel is long or short, or whether it is high, what shape the entrance to the tunnel is . . . the possibilities are endless.

Case study
Simon, aged 5, has an autistic spectrum disorder and he is extremely interested in wheels, particularly when they are spinning or turning. The practitioner, Maria, has exploited this to work with Simon on circles. She initially used the wheels of the tricycles, prams, buggies and trailers before moving to the smaller toys and equipment to help Simon to learn the characteristics of a circle. He can point to wheels in pictures and tell Maria what shape they are and is now beginning to identify circles in other contexts.

Handy hints

Help children with learning difficulties to generalise concepts of number, height, shape, length and so on by exploring the large equipment. Examples of questions you might ask include: 'How many swings are there?', 'Who is shorter / taller than the slide?', 'What shape is the trailer?', 'What's longer than the tricycle?'

Paint a mark on one tyre of an SEN child's wheelchair and let him go along an opened roll of wallpaper. He can count the number of revolutions between A and B by seeing the paint marks on the paper.

Early learning goals and large equipment activities
Time spent on large equipment activities can focus on the following early learning goals:

- Use developing mathematical ideas and methods to solve practical problems.
- In practical activities and discussions begin to use the vocabulary involved in adding and subtracting.
- Use everyday words to describe position.

Photocopiable activity sheets

It is crucially important that the children have lots of concrete experience with practical examples before they use a worksheet. Consolidation of a teaching point using worksheets must be done only when the children have thoroughly grasped the concept. If you think they still need practice with a particular maths concept, do not give them any worksheets to complete. Photocopiable Sheets 5–11 on pages 52–8 are designed to help children work on number, shape, size, pattern and colour.

Further reading

National Numeracy Strategy: Framework for Teaching Mathematics from Reception to Year 6 (DfEE, 1999).
Children and Number by Martin Hughes (Blackwell, 1986).
An Early Start to Mathematics by R. Richards and L. Jones (Simon and Schuster, 1990).

Useful addresses

The following organisations are excellent for exciting and stimulating maths equipment (and lots of other stuff too!)

LDA
Duke Street
Wisbech
Cambridgeshire PE13 2AE
Tel: 01945 463441
Fax (freephone): 0800 7838648
website: www.LDAlearning.com

Galt Educational
Johnsonbrook Road
Hyde
Cheshire SK14 4QT
Tel: 0870 242 4477
Fax (freephone): 0800 0560314

Photocopiable Sheet 5

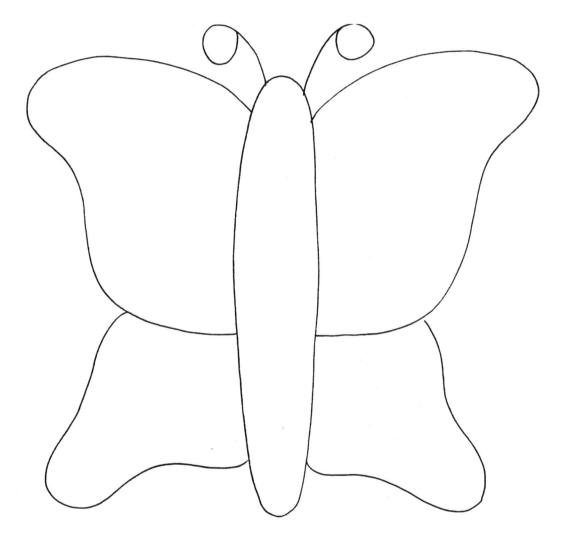

Use this sheet to work on colour, shape and/or number by helping the child to design a pattern on the wings, as required.

Photocopiable Sheet 6

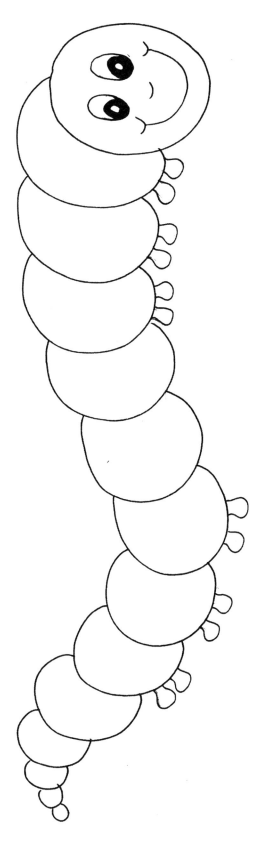

Use this sheet for patterns of colour, shape and/or number. Cut out the shape making it 'shorter' with fewer segments or 'longer' by adding more segments.

Photocopiable Sheet 7

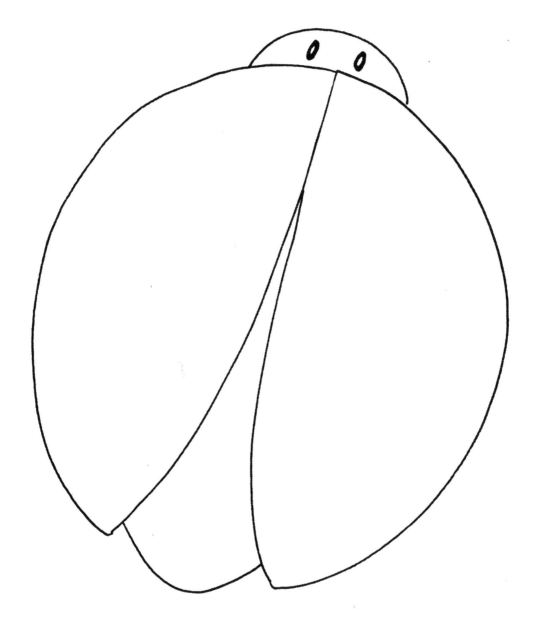

Use this sheet to work on colour, shape and/or number by helping the child to design a pattern on the wings, as required.

Photocopiable Sheet 8

Use this sheet to work on size, shape, patterns and/or colour.

Photocopiable Sheet 9

Use this sheet to work on size, shape, patterns and/or colour.

Photocopiable Sheet 10

Use this sheet to work on size, shape, patterns and/or colour.

Photocopiable Sheet 11

Use this sheet to work on size, shape, patterns and/or colour.

5   Knowledge and understanding of the world

This chapter covers:
- knowledge and understanding of the world and the special needs child
- knowledge and understanding of the world early learning goals and the special needs child
- knowledge and understanding of the world in the working areas of the setting

Knowledge and understanding of the world and the special needs child

The ability of children with SEN to develop their understanding of the world around them depends on the nature of their difficulties. For example, visually impaired children and those with dyspraxia will be challenged, because of their physical difficulties. The practitioner has to be innovative in finding ways of helping the children to use their abilities to the full. Children with learning difficulties, whether as a primary problem or as a result of another special need, are also likely to have problems with understanding their world. They will need lots of repetition before they grasp a concept, particularly if it is abstract in nature, so here the practitioner will be challenged. Because some of the areas in this part of the curriculum may be outside the children's immediate experience, we have to give them practical and concrete activities and experiences that give the teaching point some meaning. For example, history is very difficult for them – indeed time as a concept is difficult for any small children to grasp, let alone those with special needs – and information respecting history will have little or no meaning for them without practical examples and experiences.

Similarly, many SEN children have great difficulty with other abstract skills such as prediction or problem-solving. They need support and lots of practice to develop these skills, and they can have these through exciting and interesting activities that challenge their curiosity.

Knowledge and understanding of the world early learning goals and the special needs child

Exploring and observing

As practitioners, we should tap the natural urge of children to explore (starting with babies who put everything into their mouths) and use it as a resource for helping SEN children, within the parameters of their difficulties, to develop their understanding of the world. There is a wealth of tools, technology and equipment to help us do this, thus giving the children the firsthand and practical experiences they need.

Closely linked with exploring is observing – the two go hand in hand – and it's our responsibility to help the children to become aware of and refine their observation skills. Again, firsthand experience of exciting and interesting activities plays a crucial role here. Use sensitive and relevant intervention to steer SEN children towards making discoveries through their observations.

Problem-solving and predicting

These are difficult skills for SEN children to develop, because of their abstract nature. A future event, a result or an outcome are by definition non-existent, and this is what children who need concrete and physical examples, find so hard to grasp. Only with patience and by giving lots of practical experience can we make sure that SEN children increase their ability to develop these skills. By asking 'What will happen next?' and discussing possible outcomes during every activity, we will eventually involve the children in the process and, in time, they should be able to have a go themselves.

Making decisions and joining discussions

Decision-making involves a degree of prediction – when we make a decision, we guess the possible consequences and then go for the best option. So, again, when making decisions, children with SEN face the hurdle of overcoming the abstract. An extension of this is their possible difficulty in joining discussions – without the ability to predict, they may be unable to make a contribution to the general debate. As we help them to develop their problem-solving and prediction skills, they will have the confidence and ability to express their own ideas and opinions in support of a decision.

Knowledge and understanding of the world in the working areas of the setting

The home corner

Use the home corner to give SEN children 'real' experiences:

- Use Information and Communications Technology (ICT) – turn the home corner into a café and help children to design the menus and print them out, using a touch screen for those with dexterity problems; for a railway station, help visually impaired children to record the train arrivals and departures on a cassette.
- Explore other cultures, e.g. recruit a willing parent to create an ethnic home in the home corner; the physically disabled child, for example, may have less opportunity to visit other cultures' homes, temples, food stores, etc.
- Have some 'hands on' history activities, for instance make an old-fashioned kitchen (the local museum education department may well agree to lend some artefacts for authenticity), to give SEN children a concrete experience of the past – a thoroughly abstract concept to many of them.

Handy hints

☞ Do some cooking, helping the children to observe the changes that take place at each stage from mixing the ingredients to seeing the food in its final state. Involve the SEN children in the physical activity as much as possible – those with dyspraxia, visual impairment, language difficulties and learning difficulties will all benefit from this experience. Share a snack afterwards in the home corner with the newly made food.

☞ Turn the home corner into a garden with model minibeasts. Explore the insects and plants outside before doing the activity. Help the SEN children to observe and talk about the features of the insects, leaves, flowers and other natural objects during the 'research'.

▨ *Early learning goals and the home corner*

Time spent in the home corner can focus on the following early learning goals:
- Find out about and identify the uses of everyday technology and use information and communication technology and programmable toys to support their learning.
- Find out about past and present events in their own lives, and in those of their families and other people they know.
- Begin to know about their own cultures and beliefs and those of other people.
- Ask questions about why things happen and how things work.

Sand and water play

Use water play to:

- explore early scientific concepts such as temperature and consistency – use warm and cold water and adopt relevant vocabulary during discussions; use ice cubes and water to introduce 'liquid' and 'solid', letting the children experience the change as the ice melts. You may need to repeat the activities a few times to make sure that SEN children understand;
- find out about floating and sinking – drop objects into the water (e.g. pebbles, corks, screwed-up paper balls, ping-pong balls, clay, coins, etc.) and ask the visually impaired children to tell you what they sound like as they hit the water; encourage the children to play with the objects themselves and discover their floating or sinking properties.

Use sand play to:

- explore change – help the children to discover what happens to dry sand when water is added; encourage dyspraxic children or those with other physical difficulties to practise filling and pouring movements during this activity; support the children with language delay or deprivation to expand their vocabulary by discussing what they observe; encourage children with a hearing impairment to describe what they see;
- look at similarities and differences, using dry sand and wet sand with a variety of toys and tools such as a sieve, a funnel, different containers, a mill and so on;

challenge the children to find out whether wet or dry sand is the same or different with each toy; use other dry or wet substances such as flour or powdered potato to compare with the sand – do they need the same quantity of water to achieve the same wet consistency?

Handy hints

☞ If possible, let the children who work at floor level do some water play in an inflatable paddling pool to enjoy a full sensory experience, as well as exploring some of the properties of water. (Liaise with their physiotherapist and parents before doing this; they will need to be kept warm.) They may also benefit from exploring sand while playing in a sandpit.

☞ Have ready a variety of substances to mix with water and encourage the children to discover what happens when they put them together, e.g. washing-up liquid, paint, sugar, bicarbonate of soda, oil, etc. What happens if they mix the substances before adding them to the water, e.g. the paint and the washing-up liquid, or the sugar and the oil? What happens when they add the mixtures to the water?

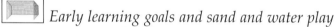 *Early learning goals and sand and water play*

Time spent in sand and water play can focus on the following early learning goals:

- Investigate objects and materials by using all of their senses as appropriate.
- Look closely at similarities, differences, patterns and change.
- Ask questions about why things happen and how things work.

The music corner

Use music to help SEN children make discoveries by:

- experimenting with the instruments in unconventional ways – baffle drums, shakers and rattles, for example, with cloths of different thickness to make new sounds, or play the instruments in unusual ways such as tapping a whistle or rubbing a drum. Involving children with autistic spectrum disorders or visual impairment in activities such as these can be very effective;
- encouraging them to feel their throats while singing, talking or whispering. What do they discover? Experiment with touching other parts of the head and face while vocalising. What can they feel when they touch someone else's throat or cheeks?
- composing their own music – this is a super way to help SEN children develop sequential memory, predicting skills ('If I bang the drum here we won't be able to hear the shaker') and language abilities. Help them to record it onto a cassette while discovering how the recorder works.

Handy hints

Let SEN children explore the instruments in their own time, encouraging them to discover how they work, e.g. by blowing, banging, shaking and so on. Through sensitive intervention, help them to expand their vocabulary. Together, make some more instruments, using junk, that are played by the newly discovered methods.

Together, make some instruments that can be hung up and played by the wind, e.g. sets of straws, tin cans, yoghurt cartons, milk bottle tops, etc. Encourage the children to discuss the different sounds they hear.

Early learning goals and the music corner

Time spent in the music corner can focus on the following early learning goals:
- Investigate objects and materials by using all of their senses as appropriate.
- Find out about, and identify, some features of . . . objects and events they observe.
- Ask questions about why things happen and how things work.

The maths area

Help SEN children to make discoveries by exploring the maths equipment in different ways:

- Have fun using the solid shapes to make constructions; help children to discover which will stay together and which fall apart; what can they use to make their constructions more stable?
- Help them to discover how they can make a shape from others, e.g. a square from two triangles or three regular rectangles, or a large triangle from four regular smaller triangles. What other patterns can they make from the shapes? (See Photocopiable Sheets 8–11 on pages 55–8.)
- Let them discover whether sets of different objects (the number they are currently working on) are heavier, lighter, or the same (e.g. two marbles, two ping-pong balls, two flowers, two pebbles, etc.) Can they guess why they are different weights? You may need to help them here, since speculating, like prediction, is an abstract skill and quite difficult for children with SEN.

Case study
Kerry, aged 5, has cerebral palsy and works both at floor level and in a supporting stand. She wanted to know what shapes she could spot in her stand, so examined it from her floor station. She identified rectangles, squares and triangles and insisted there were also circles, disagreeing with the student on work experience who was helping Kerry with the task. When the practitioner pointed out the castors at the base of the stand, Kerry's triumph over the student beamed from her big grin!

Handy hints

When exploring solid shapes, play a game where SEN children roll each one down a slope to discover which ones 'go' and which don't. According to the children's achievement levels, use only one or two shapes initially, increasing the number as they become more adept at the game. Involve the children who work at floor level by positioning the slope near them; involve those in a wheelchair by resting the slope on the chair.

Use an abacus for number exploration and explain that this was how children in former times learnt to count. An abacus is also a good way of helping visually impaired children to count since the beads can't move away or be missed. Help the children to make an abacus with beads and plant sticks: put the sticks into oasis or Plasticine and feed the beads onto them, using the number(s) that the children know. Place corks on the top of the sticks to protect the children's eyes.

Early learning goals and the maths area

Time spent in the maths area can focus on the following early learning goals:

- Find out about, and identify, some features of . . . objects and events they observe.
- Look closely at similarities, differences, patterns and change.
- Ask questions about why things happen and how things work.

The book and story corner

Books are a great resource for:

- exploring history by looking at non-fiction books showing social history; have some real examples of artefacts to illustrate various aspects; encourage the visually impaired children to use all their senses to explore these; arrange for a grandparent to come in and talk to the children about their childhood – use books that illustrate what they say;
- understanding another culture through both fiction and non-fiction; explore some ethnic recipes and if possible follow up with a cooking session, involving dyspraxic children; look at books that show the clothes and homes of other cultures – hold a 'fashion show' if parents are willing to come in and show their traditional costumes;
- presenting disability in a positive light; read stories with a character who is disabled; look at non-fiction books that give information about particular disabilities and how these can be managed in everyday living – where possible make it relevant to the SEN children in the group; if the children have any specialised equipment or aids, look at them together and discuss them; if their homes are adapted to their needs, ask the parents whether you can show photographs of these as part of the session.

Handy hints

👉 Have some persona dolls to give all the children in the setting an awareness of disability, and to present disability in a positive light. Use these together with the children when reading stories that feature a child with a disability, allowing them to explore and examine the prosthesis or equipment that goes with the doll. Leave the dolls out for the children to play with and explore.

👉 Make some books together that can be shared later. Let the children take apart an old book to see how it was made, using it as a model for their own book. Encourage them to plan the materials needed, the method of making and the content of the books.

Early learning goals and the book and story corner

Time spent in the book and story corner can focus on the following early learning goals:

- Find out about past and present events in their own lives, and in those of their families and other people they know.
- Observe, find out about and identify features in the place they live and the natural world.
- Begin to know about their own cultures and beliefs and those of other people.

The art and craft area

During art sessions:

- help SEN children to use tools and equipment – if they have physical difficulties, dexterity problems or visual impairment, for example, they may need help with learning how to use scissors, staplers, cutters and so on. You may find it useful to give them equipment that is specially adapted for children with special needs (see 'Useful addresses' at end of Chapter 6);
- explore the art of other cultures and do some work based on this, e.g. take the colours and patterns of ethnic designs and explore them together as a stimulus for new designs;
- support the children in practising techniques such as cutting, folding, joining, painting and using textural decorating. Again, they may need adapted tools for this.

Handy hints

👉 Use painting and artwork software as a complementary medium, which helps SEN children to explore and develop ICT skills at the same time.

👉 Collect 'minibeasts' from the garden and use them as the basis for artwork. Encourage SEN children to develop their observation skills and involve them in discussions about the insects. Let the children with limited vision use a magnifier to examine each insect in detail.

Early learning goals and the art and craft area

Time spent in the art and craft area can focus on the following early learning goals:

- Select the tools and techniques they need to shape, assemble and join materials they are using.
- Find out about and identify the uses of everyday technology and use information and communication technology . . . to support their learning.
- Begin to know about their own cultures and beliefs and those of other people.

Table-top activities

Use some of the table-top activities to:

- challenge SEN children to create their own games using the setting's as a model. For example, after talking about a jigsaw children might make their own by sticking a picture on card and cutting it up; having discussed the threading equipment they could make their own sets with bobbins, rings, ribbon, string and so on. Does the game work the same way as the commercially produced one?
- make maps, pictures or patterns, e.g. using the straws, blocks and beads to make a map of the setting and its playground, or a 2D model of the workroom itself;
- help the children to create the same pattern with a variety of materials, e.g. red-yellow using beads, straws, laces and pegs; or two-one-two-one with cubes, buttons, straws and rings. Can they tell you how the patterns are the same? How are they different?

Handy hints

Together, make Snap cards using different textured materials (see Photocopiable Sheet 2 on page 13). Use 'feely' materials such as velvet, sandpaper, fur and bubble wrap and stick a sample onto each card. Encourage discussions about the textures, what they are made of, how they make the game different and so on. Encourage the children to decide on the tools and equipment needed to make the cards.

When playing board games, talk about the rules and encourage discussions about how they make the games successful. Can the SEN children think of a new rule that helps the game along? Experiment with it and try again if it doesn't work – this introduces the idea of making a theory, trying it out and then rethinking if necessary.

 Early learning goals and table-top activities

Time spent on table-top activities can focus on the following early learning goals:
- Investigate objects and materials by using all of their senses as appropriate.
- Look closely at similarities, differences, patterns and change.
- Find out about their environment, and talk about those features they like and dislike.

Small equipment activities

Help SEN children to make discoveries by:

- using the same equipment indoors and out, exploring how they work differently: 'What happens to a ball rolled along the smooth floor and then bumpy ground?', 'What happens when a hoop is rolled along the floor and then through a puddle?', 'What happens when a ping-pong ball is thrown up indoors and then outside on a windy day?'
- using the equipment in different ways: 'What happens when a bat touches/pushes/taps/hits a ball?', 'What happens when a skipping-rope is turned/shaken/flicked/dragged, by one person and then two?'
- using different equipment in the same way: 'What happens when a ball/a beanbag/a rope/a hoop is hit with a hand and then with a bat?', 'What happens when a beanbag/a ball/a skipping-rope is sent down a slope?, What happens when these things are kicked?'

Handy hints

Change the equipment slightly to explore how the game is affected when played differently. For instance, play skittles with tins, plastic bottles, small bricks or cartons as skittles; play football with beanbags; play skipping-rope games with large hoops.

Help SEN children to invent new games. For example, tie a large hoop horizontally between two posts before throwing beanbags through it; mark out a target area on the floor with ropes (choose the size according to the children's needs) for balls or beanbags; lay bats on the floor and throw hoops to land over the bats.

 *Early learning goals and small equipment activities*
Time spent on small equipment activities can focus on the following early learning goals:
- Investigate objects and materials by using all of their senses as appropriate.
- Ask questions about why things happen and how things work.

Large equipment activities

Use the large equipment to:

- set SEN children problem-solving tasks, encouraging them to work out and try solutions, e.g. 'How can we make a bridge across this "river", using the . . . and the . . . ?' or 'What will happen if we put the blocks across here before we ride the tricycle?' This can be difficult for SEN children because it involves prediction and planning, both abstract skills that are often challenging;
- encourage the children's awareness of safety aspects – let them explore some of the equipment and talk to them about why there are safety features or how we need to play on them carefully. This is a type of prediction and speculation that SEN children may find difficult and will need to have experience of;

• provide a pattern for making models that they can use in small-people play. The children will have to explore how the equipment works, decide on the materials they need to make a copy and then build their own versions for the Play People.

Case study
Polly, aged 5, is visually impaired and lacked confidence on the climbing frame. Josh, a sixth-former on work experience, helped Polly to become familiar with the frame, but she was still anxious about how high she had climbed. Josh attached differently textured materials to each rung and section of the frame and then spent time with Polly helping her to discover the newly marked equipment. She quickly learnt to recognise where she was on the frame and would then decide whether to climb further or come down again. Before Josh had finished his placement, Polly was happily playing on the frame, using the markers as her guidelines.

Handy hints

Help the children to explore how a wheelchair works as compared with a tricycle, a buggy or a trailer. Involve children who work from a wheelchair, by encouraging them to tell and show the others how to manoeuvre it.

Use the large blocks to make a 3D 'ground map' of the room, street or playground. SEN children may need quite a bit of support in this, since to transfer the image of a real object to a representative model can be difficult. If they find it hard, make the map show a small and very familiar area, such as another part of the place they are currently working in, so they can refer to it instantly while they build.

Early learning goals and large equipment activities
Time spent on large equipment activities can focus on the following early learning goals:
• Investigate objects and materials by using all of their senses as appropriate.
• Ask questions about why things happen and how things work.
• Build and construct with a wide range of objects, selecting appropriate resources, and adapting their work where necessary.

Further reading

Outdoor Play in the Early Years: Management and Innovation by Helen Bilton (David Fulton Publishers, 2001).
Planning an Appropriate Curriculum for the Under Fives by Rosemary Rodger (David Fulton Publishers, 1999).

Useful addresses

Hope Education
Orb Mill
Huddersfield Road
Waterhead, Oldham
Lancashire OL4 2ST
Tel: 0161 633 6611
Fax: 0161 633 3431
email: enquiries@hope-education.co.uk

6 Physical development

This chapter covers:
- physical development and the special needs child
- physical development early learning goals and the special needs child
- physical development in the working areas of the setting

Physical development and the special needs child

Physical development is not a separate 'subject', but is an integral part of children's overall development, affecting everything they do, whether or not they have SEN. It involves a close relationship between movement, learning and language, and SEN children may experience difficulties in any, or all, of these. The type of difficulty experienced by children will naturally affect their physical development; a visually impaired child, for example, will have different problems from a child who works from a wheelchair, and both of these children will experience different problems from a child who is able-bodied but who has emotional difficulties.

Gross motor skills

Gross motor skills develop as children learn to move with their bodies, heads, arms and legs. The larger movements involved in wider activities are all part of gross motor development. Children need to learn how to run, jump, climb, catch, throw, propel wheeled toys, hop, skip and so on. Plan carefully for the children who have physical, sensory and/or motor difficulties. Developing gross motor skills is the first stage towards developing fine motor skills.

Fine motor skills

The development of fine motor skills involves the children's successful use of their fingers, thumbs and hands. The ability to perform small movements such as grasp and release, pinching, threading, cutting, pouring, sticking, squeezing, writing, painting and so on, is crucial for the development of children's self-help skills, including washing hands, putting on a coat, doing up buttons or tying laces. Fingers and thumbs need as much exercise and practice as legs and feet. Children with dyspraxia will need lots of support and practice here.

Spatial awareness

By practising both gross and fine movements, children develop spatial awareness that gives them a sense of where they are, in relation to both other people and their immediate environment. They need to develop spatial awareness in order to understand what's going on around them, thereby making them balanced and giving them a sense of well-being. SEN children may need a little extra help in refining these movements, and in doing spatial awareness activities.

Physical development early learning goals and the special needs child

When Give SEN children lots of time to explore and experiment without pressure so that they can persist in achieving a difficult goal.

Where Both indoors and out, make space available where a range of activities and experiences can be offered.

How Provide equipment that will challenge the children; if they have physical and/or motor difficulties, liaise with the occupational therapist or physiotherapist; if they have a sensory impairment, work with the appropriate support services.

What Make the language of movement an integral part of any activity; provide opportunities for the children to experience large and small movements, to develop confidence and control, and to learn how to keep themselves safe.

Physical development in the working areas of the setting

The home corner

Have fun practising fine motor skills in the home corner. Explore health and safety issues when the opportunity arises:

- Dressing up involves buttoning and unbuttoning, zipping and unzipping, fastening and unfastening (maybe haphazardly, but hand movements will be involved), pulling up and taking down and so on.
- 'Cooking' involves pouring, squeezing, mixing, stirring, cutting and rolling – all important actions for muscle tone and strengthening, coordination, crossing the midline and so on.
- Using the telephone, the television, the iron and the washing machine in the house, all provide useful manipulation exercises.
- Imaginative play can lead to discussion of the importance of cleanliness, eating sensibly and getting enough sleep; SEN children need lots of repetition and practice to assimilate information and skills, so bringing these issues into home corner play will help to reinforce them.

Handy hints

☞ Use dressing up games, and activities with a routine such as making dinner, to help dyspraxic children develop ordering skills, something that often needs to be worked on.

☞ Baking – particularly making dough, which is a more 'hands on' activity – is useful for developing fine motor skills. Children who are visually impaired or have physical difficulties or dyspraxia will benefit here.

▨ *Early learning goals and the home corner*

Time spent in the home corner can focus on the following early learning goals:

- Move with control and coordination.
- Use a range of small and large equipment.
- Handle tools, objects, construction and malleable materials safely and with increasing control.
- Recognise the importance of keeping healthy and those things which contribute to this.

Sand and water play

Help SEN children to develop fine motor skills, coordination and muscle tone by encouraging them to:

- squeeze water through large syringes, funnels or tubes, or pour water from container to container (scent the water for the children with visual problems); use sponges in the water for the children to squeeze;
- pour dry sand through funnels, tubes or sieves, or from container to container;
- squeeze, pat and push wet sand while making sand castles or pies;
- mix water and sand, making a 'dough' and squeezing it into shape.

Handy hints

☞ Pour a colour into the water tray (at one end only) and encourage the SEN children to swirl it around with their hands and/or an implement, to practise dexterity, coordination, hand dominance, crossing the midline and strengthening muscle tone.

☞ Challenge the children to pour dry sand, holding the container at different heights. This helps them to practise hand–eye coordination and spatial awareness, maintain a grasp for longer periods, and strengthen their arm and hand muscles.

Early learning goals and sand and water play
Time spent in sand and water play can focus on the following early learning goals:
- Move with control and coordination.
- Show awareness of space, of themselves and of others.
- Use a range of small and large equipment.
- Handle tools, objects, construction and malleable materials safely and with increasing control.

The music corner

Music is excellent for helping to develop rhythm, which is an important part of movement and coordination. Encourage children to:

- move in different ways to appropriate music, e.g. marching, creeping, jumping, etc.;
- dance freely to a range of musical styles; if the children are in a wheelchair or a brace, encourage them to move their arms and upper body to the music;
- clap and/or jump to different tempos and beats; if some find that clapping is difficult, attach a bell or a rattle to their hand with Velcro and encourage them to move their hand to the beat;
- play the keyboard instruments, shakers and clappers, either freely or in time to a piece of music.

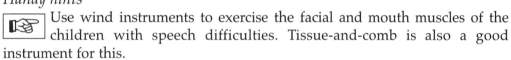

Handy hints
Use wind instruments to exercise the facial and mouth muscles of the children with speech difficulties. Tissue-and-comb is also a good instrument for this.

Make a carton into a drum for the children who have fine motor difficulties, to create a larger surface area for them to hit, either with their hands or a stick as appropriate.

 Early learning goals and the music corner
Time spent in the music corner can focus on the following early learning goals:
- Move with control and coordination.
- Handle tools, objects, construction and malleable materials safely and with increasing control.

The maths area

Use work on number to practise motor skills by:

- counting strides, hops, rolls, jumps, hoops crawled through, throws, catches, and other movements;
- counting beads as they are threaded, the quantity of pegs clipped onto a box, the number of Jack straws picked up, how many squeezes of a washing-up bottle it takes to empty it of water and so on.

Exploit weighing and measuring by:

- challenging children with dexterity problems to tip the scales with beads picked up and dropped into the pan, or to pour water into different containers to judge capacity;
- challenging children in a wheelchair to propel themselves further than a given point, or dyspraxic children to walk along a bench before measuring with string how far they go each time – can they beat their own record?
- challenging children to complete a required movement on large equipment (around, under, over, through, etc.) before a sand-timer runs out.

Handy hints

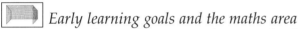 When working on a specific number with children who have difficulties with fine motor movements, encourage them to make lots of sets of that number with beads, cubes or buttons. They will be practising counting the number and also the grasp-and-release movement.

Use sorting, matching and pattern-making activities to practise pointing, grasp and release, pincer actions, crossing the midline, and similar movements.

Early learning goals and the maths area

Time spent in the maths area can focus on the following early learning goals:
- Move with control and coordination.
- Travel around, under, over and through balancing and climbing equipment.
- Use a range of large and small equipment.

The book and story corner

Use the book and story corner to:

- practise gross motor skills by acting scenes from traditional stories and rhymes, e.g. *Jack and the Beanstalk* (giant striding), *The Three Little Pigs* (wolf climbing onto the roof), *The Gingerbread Man* (running), *The Grand Old Duke of York* (marching), and the cow jumping over the moon;
- practise fine motor skills, again, by acting out traditional stories and rhymes (e.g. Rumpelstiltskin spinning the straw, the shoemaker sewing the elves' shoes, baking a cake (*Pat-a-cake, Pat-a-cake, baker man*), winding the bobbin and so on;
- explore action rhymes;
- find the 'health and safety' elements in a story (e.g. wandering off alone (*Goldilocks*), needing food, warmth and shelter (*Hansel and Gretel*), etc.).

Handy hints

☞ Help the children to make props to use in their acting sessions, e.g. apples for Snow White, fat sausages to sizzle, sewing kits for the shoemaker, Humpty Dumpty's wall, etc. Both making and then using these will help develop motor skills.

☞ Together make up some action rhymes and stories. The rhymes don't have to rhyme and can be as silly as the children like, as long as they have action and movement elements. You could also extend a favourite (published) action poem by making up extra verses.

Early learning goals and the book and story corner

Time spent in the book and story corner can focus on the following early learning goals:
- Move with confidence, imagination and in safety.
- Move with control and coordination.
- Recognise the importance of keeping healthy and those things which contribute to this.

The art and craft area

Art and craft helps physical development through:

- using scissors, paintbrushes, crayons, glue sticks, etc. (see Chapter 1 for suggestions for adapting tools for some SEN children);
- squeezing, rolling, pulling and pinching malleable materials; finger-painting, model-making and so on;
- using other materials such as bubble wrap, different texture fabrics, scrunched up newspaper, cold cooked spaghetti, pulses, etc.;
- making models – using larger cartons also helps to develop spatial awareness;
- doing 'temporary art', e.g. 'painting' the playground using a large brush, or a sponge, and water, or making sculptures with foam or mousse;
- learning about personal safety issues through the use of scissors, modelling sticks and other potentially harmful equipment.

Case study

Gareth, aged 5, has dyspraxia and needs to strengthen the muscles in his hands. He and Lydia, the Learning Support Assistant, made papier mâché using flour and water (mixed by Gareth) and strips of newspaper (torn by Gareth), which he then placed around an inflated balloon. When the papier mâché was dry, Gareth and Lydia painted a face on it, after taking out the balloon. Gareth's hand muscles, two-handed coordination and hand–eye coordination were all exercised in this activity.

Handy hints

☞ Make thicker jelly than usual by adding less water, for the children who need practice in squeezing but who find conventional malleable materials too difficult. As their muscle tone improves, give them more challenging materials to work on.

☞ Make ice cubes with different coloured waters. Help the children take them out of the cases and make patterns. What happens when they melt? Challenge them to swirl all the colours together with their hands and/or an implement.

▦ *Early learning goals and the art and craft area*
Time spent in the art and craft area can focus on the following early learning goals:
• Move with control and coordination.
• Show awareness of space, of themselves and of others.
• Handle tools, objects, construction and malleable materials safely and with increasing control.
• Recognise the importance of keeping healthy and those things which contribute to this.

Table-top activities

Get the children to play at:

• threading – by using big beads, buttons and lacing cards; for the children who have difficulties with this, make jumbo 'beads' using cut-up cardboard tubes;
• pinching – by clipping clothes pegs onto a rope, the edge of a box or a tray; or by practising picking up objects and dropping them into a box using thumb and forefinger as chopsticks; and also popping bubble wrap;
• grasping and releasing – by using posting toys, large jigsaws, a feely bag or a feely box full of favourite toys, etc.;
• pulling apart and pushing together – by using toys such as Duplo, Lego or stickle bricks;
• pointing – by using tracking toys, toys with buttons or switches, or finger puppets (see Photocopiable Sheet 4 on page 40);
• tracking with a jumbo pencil (see Photocopiable Sheets 12–14 on pages 81–3).

Handy hints

☞ To practise grasp and release, use dry pasta shapes starting with the larger types, e.g. lasagne, gradually moving to smaller shapes. Cannelloni makes good 'big beads' for threading, and as skills become more refined, use penne or macaroni. For added practice, the child can paint the pasta before use.

☞ Make a 'custom-built' posting box, with the size of the hole and the objects to be posted based on the children's ability levels. As their skills improve, reduce the size of the hole.

Early learning goals and table-top activities

Time spent on table-top activities can focus on the following early learning goals:
- Handle tools, objects, construction and malleable materials safely and with increasing control.
- Move with control and coordination.

Small equipment activities

- Use a row of horizontal hoops to practise jumping, and vertical hoops to practise crawling – coordination, special awareness and muscle tone will all benefit.
- Mark a start/finish point on the largest hoop available and ask the children with visual impairment or physical difficulties to move their hands around the hoop's circumference, with arms stretched as far as possible.
- Use bats, balls, beanbags, etc. to help children in a wheelchair to develop the muscles of their upper bodies. Check with the physiotherapist for appropriate activities for lower body muscle tone.
- Suspend bells, rattles and shakers from string stretched across a gap. Encourage the children who work at floor level to hit them until they make a sound.

Case study

Nigel, aged 4, is confined to a wheelchair because his leg bones are gradually disintegrating. He loves football, so the practitioner and the group devised a version of the game that meant Nigel could join in. They use a soft ball and play in the hall. The rules of the game stay the same except the players use hands instead of feet. Nigel's skill at propelling his chair around has increased remarkably and his throwing and catching abilities outstrip many of the able-bodied children!

Handy hints

 Make an alley with large blocks so the child with physical or sensory difficulties can join a game of skittles or 'roll for a goal' with a soft ball without losing the ball.

 Attach lengths of string to beanbags, quoits etc. so that the visually impaired child can throw and then retrieve them. Make sure the string is longer than he can throw and that the other end is attached to his wrist.

 Early learning goals and small equipment activities

Time spent on small equipment activities can focus on the following early learning goals:
- Move with control and coordination.
- Show awareness of space, of themselves and of others.
- Use a range of large and small equipment.

Large equipment activities

Play on large equipment is ideal for:

- helping children with dyspraxia or physical difficulties to work on gross movements;
- helping children with visual impairment to push, pull, climb, crawl and so on with confidence;
- helping children with sequencing problems to practise set sequences, starting with two consecutive movements and gradually increasing the number of elements in a sequence;
- exploring how activity causes bodily changes, what these are and why; SEN children may not be aware of these, so use large equipment play to talk together about them;
- exploring issues of keeping healthy and safe.

See Figure 6.1 for a suggested layout of large apparatus for outdoor play, to give SEN children with physical difficulties a range of movement opportunities.

Handy hints

☞ Use a parachute for lots of fun with running, crawling, hopping, rolling and so on. Several children hold its edge and move their arms up and down, making the silk billow, while the other children have to cross under it before it floats back down.

☞ Give the visually impaired children the opportunity to experiment safely and with confidence on tricycles and with buggies. Start with a limited area and, as they gain confidence, increase this. Encourage the other children to be sensitive to them, as they experiment with and learn the perimeters of the play area.

Early learning goals and large equipment activities
Time spent on large equipment activities can focus on the following early learning goals:
- Move with confidence, imagination and in safety.
- Move with control and coordination.
- Travel around, under, over and through balancing and climbing equipment.
- Show awareness of space, of themselves and of others.
- Recognise the importance of keeping healthy and those things which contribute to this.
- Recognise the changes that happen to their bodies when they are active.

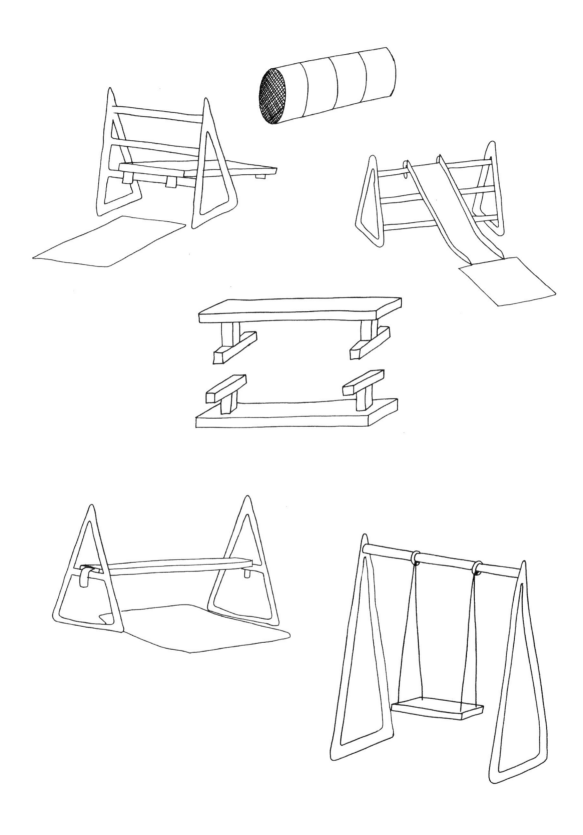

Figure 6.1 Example of layout for large equipment play

Photocopiable activity sheets

It is crucially important that children have lots of concrete experience with practical examples before they use a worksheet. Consolidation of a teaching point using worksheets must be done only when the children have thoroughly grasped the concept. If you think they still need practice with a particular skill, do not give them any worksheets to complete.

Further reading

Fingers and Thumbs: Toys and Activities for Children with Hand-function Problems by Roma Lear (Butterworth Heinemann, 1999).
Dyspraxia in the Early Years by Christine Macintyre (David Fulton Publishers, 2000).
Small Steps Forward: Using Games and Activities to Help Your Pre-School Child with Special Needs by Sarah Newman (Jessica Kingsley Publishers, 1999).

Useful addresses

National Association of Toy and Leisure Libraries
68 Churchway
London NW1 1LT
Tel: 020 7387 9592
Fax: 020 7383 2714
email: admin@natll.ukf.net

Nottingham Rehab
Findel House
Excelsior Road
Ashby Park
Ashby
Leicestershire LE65 1NG
Tel: 0870 600 197
Fax: 01530 419 150

Fledglings
6 Southfield
Ickleton
Saffron Walden
CB10 1TE
Tel: 0845 458 1124
Fax: 0845 458 1125
email: enquiries@fledglings.org.uk

ROMPA
Goyt Side Road
Chesterfield
Derbyshire S40 2PH
Tel: 0800 056 2323
Fax: 01246 221802
email: sales@rompa.co.uk
website: www.rompa.co.uk

TFH
5–7 Severnside Business Park
Severn Road
Stourport-on-Severn
Worcestershire DY13 9HT
Tel: 01299 827820
Fax: 01299 827035
email: tfh@tfhuk.com
website: www.tfhuk.com

Photocopiable Sheet 12

Use this sheet to practise tracking and fine motor skills.

Photocopiable Sheet 13

Use this sheet to practise tracking and fine motor skills.

Photocopiable Sheet 14

Use this sheet to practise tracking and fine motor skills.

7 Creative development

This chapter covers:
- creative development and the special needs child
- creative development early learning goals and the special needs child
- creative development in the working areas of the setting

Creative development and the special needs child

As with all areas of the Early Years curriculum, creative development cannot be regarded as isolated – it is integrated with all aspects of children's learning and is a crucial part of their whole development.

The practitioner needs to be sensitive to the children's limitations and to ensure that she provides them with every opportunity to be creative, even if this means engineering situations and/or the learning environment. For example, part of creative development means using the senses, which, for children with sensory impairments, can be difficult – activities involving sounds and sights may be less meaningful to children with visual and hearing problems. This is where the practitioner will be challenged when she plans and carries out these activities making sure the SEN children are fully included.

It is also important to remember that creative development doesn't necessarily mean the production of something tangible – making up and telling stories or poems, joining in role-play, or sharing exploratory discussions are all creative activities. These can be difficult for SEN children, because they are language-based and also abstract, but they are vital elements in both creative and overall development.

It is crucial to create an atmosphere in the setting where the children's attempts at creativity and originality are acknowledged and valued. Their achievements must be judged in the context of their abilities and the degree of effort made, and should be celebrated openly. This will also contribute to ensuring that *all* the children foster a respect of everyone's contributions regardless of ability level.

Creative development early learning goals and the special needs child

For special needs children to have optimum opportunities to develop their creative skills and aim for the early learning goals in creative development, we as practitioners need to look at how we make sure those opportunities arise. Where they do not occur naturally, we may have to engineer the situation. There are several aspects to this.

The setting

The setting may have to be adapted to ensure that SEN children can access every creative opportunity. (For a fuller discussion of this, see Chapter 1.) As practitioners we need to be tuned in to each child's difficulties, and to be innovative and flexible to ensure that all their needs are met.

For special needs children particularly, time is vital. They must be allowed to work on and complete a creative activity without being pressurised by time constraints. They may even need to repeat an activity several times, or take more time to refine their ideas, so it's important that they can have all the time they want for this.

The activities

Exciting and stimulating activities encourage children to be creative, but they must be appropriate. For example, children with autistic spectrum disorders may be overwhelmed by bright displays and lots of stimulating things to do, or those who have developmental delay may not be ready to cope with what's on offer. This is where the practitioner's sensitivity to the child is vital – the activity must be tailored to the child's needs, but must be challenging at the same time.

The opportunities

We must offer many opportunities that lend themselves to creativity – use music, art and craft, poems and stories, dance and drama and imaginative play to give children a chance to discover and develop their creative abilities.

Organise trips and visits outside the setting; arrange for creative professionals to come into the setting and share their skills with the children; hold workshops and invite the parents to come in and have a go alongside the children; invite older children into the setting to do some joint creative work; exploit the outside environment, the hall or gym, for creative ideas and activities. For each activity you organise, challenge yourself to make sure that you are including the SEN children according to their needs, enabling their creative skills to be developed to the full.

Creative development in the working areas of the setting

The home corner

Develop imaginative play by:

- joining in role-play and acting out narratives. Use familiar stories and scenarios (SEN children need this as a starting point) and gradually add creative elements, e.g. play at the seven dwarfs in their house and then begin to make up new parts to the story;
- using children's experiences to create imaginative play, e.g. 'make' a pretend cake for a birthday party, discussing what's needed and how it's done; encourage children to then plan and arrange the party invitations and games, and then hold the party;
- using the dressing up box to create characters and a story around them; it can be nonsense, as long as children's creative and imaginative skills are being challenged.

Handy hints

☞ Use a role-play based on an SEN child's experience, but cast him in a different role, e.g. a visit to the doctor where he is the doctor rather than the patient, or getting lost at the shops where he is the parent rather than the lost child. You may need to help him to work out how to play the character.

☞ Have fun changing characters in familiar stories and acting new versions, e.g. make the ugly sisters kind and gentle, Cinderella bossy and the Prince reluctant to marry Cinderella.

Early learning goals and the home corner

Time spent in the home corner can focus on the following early learning goals:

• Use their imagination in . . . imaginative and role play and stories.
• Express and communicate their ideas, thoughts and feelings by using . . . imaginative and role play . . .

Sand and water play

Creative development can be stimulated by:

• encouraging SEN children to explore how different materials react in water, e.g. paper, plastic, cloth, sandpaper, ice cubes, cotton wool, washing-up liquid, bicarbonate of soda and so on. Help visually impaired children to express their discoveries in terms of their other senses;
• designing and trying out new toys for water play. Help the children to choose appropriate materials, make the toys and then experiment with them in the water;
• experimenting with other materials and sand, e.g. glue, water, flour, paint (wet and dry), etc. Encourage the children to see what happens when they use the sand mix in other ways, such as painting with the sand-glue mix or pouring the sand-flour mix through funnels and sieves.

Handy hints

☞ Make cubes (Photocopiable Sheet 1 on page 12) and help the children to paint glue 'tracks' on the faces. Roll the cube through dry sand, dry sand-paint mix, or sand-flour mix. What happens?

☞ Help the children to 'dribble' dry and then wet sand over a variety of surfaces such as bubble wrap, sandpaper, clingfilm, foil, etc. What happens? Try the same experiment with smears of undiluted washing-up liquid on each surface. What happens?

Early learning goals and sand and water play

Time spent in sand and water play can focus on the following early learning goals:

- Explore colour, texture, shape, form and space in two or three dimensions.
- Respond in a variety of ways to what they see, hear, smell, touch and feel.
- Express and communicate their ideas, thoughts and feelings by using a widening range of materials, suitable tools ... designing and making ...

The music corner

Making music is a super medium for:

- encouraging creativity in children with a variety of special needs, including sensory impairments, physical difficulties, autistic spectrum disorders, language delay or disability, learning difficulties and emotional and/or behavioural problems. (Music therapy is now recognised as a successful medium for working with people who have difficulties.)
- integrating other creative activities such as dance, movement, mime and drama. Help SEN children explore different ways of playing instruments, moving to their sounds and composing music. (See Chapter 1 for some suggestions about using music.)
- helping to develop other important skills such as listening, memory, sequencing and rhythm. These all come into play during creative sessions and they are vital for other areas of development.

Case study

Simon, aged 4, is autistic and finds difficulty in participating in group activities. His practitioner found him under the table one day listening intently to a cassette of Enya's music. She used this later in a small group movement and dance session, encouraging Simon to join in. While he didn't dance *with* the other children, he tolerated their presence while he danced alongside them, which was a breakthrough for him.

Handy hints

Make and use instruments that vibrate so that children with sensory impairment can be involved (see Chapter 1). Even banging a wooden table with wooden or metal spoons creates sound that can be appreciated by the children.

Help the children to compose, practise and play their own music. If possible, make up a dance to accompany the piece. When they are confident, arrange to give a performance for parents, other children and/or the school. The boost in self-esteem of a child with special needs is amazing to see!

Early learning goals and the music corner
Time spent in the music corner can focus on the following early learning goals:
- Recognise and explore how sounds can be changed, sing simple songs from memory, recognise repeated sounds and sound patterns and match movements to music.
- Use their imagination in art and design, music, dance, imaginative and role play and stories.
- Express and communicate their ideas, thoughts and feelings by using . . . a variety of songs and musical instruments.

The maths area

Much of the standard maths equipment lends itself to creative work; indeed there is often an overlap between maths and creativity, e.g. pattern-making – is it maths or a creative activity?

Have some creative fun with maths by:

- using tessellated shapes to make kaleidoscope-type pictures (if appropriate, you could reinforce the concepts of colour and shape at the same time). Make some tessellated shapes from differently textured materials so that visually impaired children can feel where one shape finishes and the next begins;
- designing and making a mini seesaw to explore the concept of weight – use light and heavy objects on the seesaw and reinforce the vocabulary at the same time;
- experimenting with mixing colours – again there is an overlap: colour as a mathematical concept dovetails with colour as a creative/art medium;
- encouraging the children to design patterns using colour, shape and numbers. Those with learning and/or language difficulties may need extra help with this activity; children with autistic spectrum disorders may be very good at doing it.

Handy hints
When working on a specific number, help the children to make the numeral in lots of different sizes, colours and textures and then have fun creating pictures, patterns and collages with them. Use the vocabulary of size, colour and texture while doing this.

Encourage the children to explore some of the maths equipment as a creative medium, e.g. pose problems such as 'How can we make a . . . with these counting blocks?', 'Let's see if we can design a sausage-machine with these solid shapes' or 'What could we pretend all these beads are?'

 Early learning goals and the maths area
Time spent in the maths area can focus on the following early learning goals:
- Explore colour, texture, shape, form and space in two or three dimensions.
- Respond in a variety of ways to what they see, hear, smell, touch and feel.
- Express and communicate their ideas, thoughts and feelings by using a widening range of materials, suitable tools . . . designing and making . . .

2a2

222a2

The book and story corner

The language element in creative development is crucial for SEN children, and books, poems and stories offer many super opportunities to help them.

Have creative fun by:

- singing nursery rhymes with alternative words chosen by the children (with a little help, perhaps!), e.g. 'Humpty Dumpty sat on a donkey' or 'Woof Woof, Black Dog, have you any bones?'
- making up different endings to, or extending or mixing up elements of familiar stories, e.g. *Cinderella and the Three Bears* or *Goldilocks and the Beanstalk*;
- using poetry to make up new rhythms, rhymes and patterns – they can be nonsense words and sounds, which will encourage SEN children to have a go, since there is no pressure to get it 'right' in this game;
- making up and performing dramas together, which are based on poems, stories or rhymes, making sure SEN children are involved at each stage.

Case study
Liam, aged 5, has speech difficulties and dislikes speaking in front of others. When working with Emily, the LSA, in a one-to-one situation, he enjoys making up alternative endings to nursery rhymes. Emily helped Liam to design and make a mask, which he then wore while reciting his new rhymes. He was persuaded to share his rhymes with the others like this and he was a great hit. He is gradually joining group discussions without the mask, as his confidence grows.

Handy hints
If the budget will run to it, invite a performance poet in – they are past masters at stimulating the children's creative forces and are well worth the fee! If you give them advance warning of the particular special needs in the setting, they will plan activities accordingly.

Help the children to record their stories or poems onto a cassette and encourage them to listen to it often. Let them make changes and re-record if they wish – this encourages the idea of drafting and redrafting, which is an important part of the creative process, and also stimulates more creativity.

Early learning goals and the book and story corner
Time spent in the book and story corner can focus on the following early learning goals:
- Recognise and explore how sounds can be changed, sing simple songs from memory, recognise repeated sounds and sound patterns . . .
- Use their imagination in . . . imaginative and role play and stories.
- Express and communicate their ideas, thoughts and feelings by using . . . imaginative and role play . . . and a variety of songs.

The art and craft area

Stimulate creative ideas in art and craft by:

- bringing the outside indoors – encourage the children to explore the effects of painting on leaves, sticks, flowers, stones, moss and other natural objects. Which will stick together with glue? Which will stick to paper, plastic, wood or metal?
- taking the indoors outside – give the playground a facelift with displays of stones painted by the children, trees and shrubs decorated with bunting or streamers designed and made by the children, or sculptures designed and created by the children;
- using unconventional tools and materials, e.g. a toothbrush or a feather for painting, shredded leaves (fresh and/or dried) for textured effects or cloth as an alternative background to paper for pictures.

Handy hints

☞ Check whether children with autistic spectrum disorders have an aversion to or a fascination with any particular colour or texture. In the former case, avoid using that colour or texture during art sessions, until they have settled and are ready to be introduced to working with it; in the second case, exploit their love of the colour or texture to encourage them to be imaginative in their ideas.

☞ Dedicate a wall or part of a wall, from child-eye height to the floor, where the children are free to experiment with graffiti using different media. Cover the wall with lining paper or the reverse of wallpaper for their mark-making – you can then replace it easily when it becomes full. Make sure the children who work at floor level have the opportunity to add their contributions to the mural.

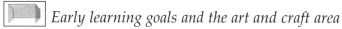 *Early learning goals and the art and craft area*

Time spent in the art and craft area can focus on the following early learning goals:
- Explore colour, texture, shape, form and space in two or three dimensions.
- Use their imagination in art and design . . .
- Express and communicate their ideas, thoughts and feelings using a widening range of materials, suitable tools, designing and making . . .

Table-top activities

Encourage creativity using table-top resources to:

- experiment with pattern-making, e.g. using pegs, straws or small blocks, with colour, shape or number; encourage the children to tell you which ones to use to continue the pattern;
- design and make models using the construction games. SEN children could begin from their own experience before creating imaginary designs, e.g. help them to make a model of a car and then discuss how to turn it into a flying machine;

- help the children to play in creative ways, e.g. use Jack straws to make a nest, or laces to weave patterns.

Handy hints

☞ If children have difficulty in picking up construction straws, put a length of fuse wire inside them, seal each end of the straw with sticky tape, and let the children use a magnet to lift them. They can then continue to make their creative constructions a little more easily.

☞ Stick Velcro on one face of construction blocks to help children with dyspraxia or other coordination difficulties to make a tower – the blocks will stick together and the tower won't fall over as easily.

Early learning goals and table-top activities
Time spent on table-top activities can focus on the following early learning goals:
- Explore colour, texture, shape, form and space in two or three dimensions.
- Express and communicate their ideas, thoughts and feelings by using a widening range of materials, suitable tools . . . designing and making . . .

Small equipment activities

Encourage creative ideas by:

- challenging the children to make up new games using different pieces of equipment in conjunction, e.g. throwing beanbags into hoops or throwing hoops over skittles. According to the needs of the children, restrict the range and number of pieces of equipment, to avoid overload;
- using pieces of small equipment to stimulate artistic creativity, e.g. making mobiles within a hoop that is suspended from the ceiling or drawing around table tennis bats before filling in the outline with different textured materials such as lentils, sand or velvet;
- using the small equipment in other working areas to stimulate the children's ideas for games and activities, e.g. putting beanbags ('rubble') into a trailer, cycling to a hoop and emptying the beanbags into the 'rubbish tip' (i.e. the hoop).

Handy hints

☞ Make beanbags from differently textured fabrics, e.g. velvet, sacking, cotton, fake fur, etc. to give a sensory experience in games and activities.

☞ Encourage the children to use pieces of small equipment as props in imaginative play, e.g. a bat as a guitar, a ball as an egg or a skittle as a bottle of milk. Ask them to talk about their ideas with you.

Early learning goals and small equipment activities
Time spent on small equipment activities can focus on the following early learning goals:
- Explore colour, texture, shape, form and space in two and three dimensions.
- Use their imagination in . . . imaginative and role play . . .
- Respond in a variety of ways to what they see, hear, smell, touch and feel.

Large equipment activities

Encourage creative play by:

- discussing with the children how some pieces of equipment could be used in imaginative play, e.g. the tricycles and trailer for Cinderella's coach or the climbing frame for the beanstalk. Use familiar stories or scenarios at first, then encourage the SEN children to incorporate some imaginative elements;
- experimenting with different equipment that isn't usually played with together, e.g. mixing outdoor and indoor apparatus or using a wheelbarrow or buggy as a trailer; encourage the children to tell you what happens;
- helping the children to use the equipment in imaginative ways, e.g. climbing up the slide, sitting on the tricycle back to front or lying on their tummies on the swing. What happens?
- doing some 'dance' routines to music, using tricycles, buggies, scooters and so on, or designing some creative gymnastics movements set to music.

Handy hints
To help the visually impaired children feel secure and confident in trying new experiences on the large apparatus, let them play on it alone first (with you supervising) so that they don't have the rough and tumble of the other children to deal with simultaneously. They could do this for a few minutes before the session begins and as they gain in confidence, encourage them to join in the inclusive play.

Liaise with the parents and/or physiotherapist of physically disabled children to plan ways of ensuring that they are able to play on the large equipment in ways that help their creativity.

 Early learning goals and large equipment activities
Time spent on large equipment activities can focus on the following early learning goals:
- Respond in a variety of ways to what they see, hear, smell, touch and feel.
- Express and communicate their ideas, thoughts and feelings by using a widening range of materials, suitable tools . . . [and] movement.

Further reading

Pre-school and Infant Art by K. Jameson (Studio Vista, 1974).
Making Music with the Young Child with Special Needs by E. Streeter (Jessica Kingsley Publishers, 1993).

Useful addresses

British Society for Music Therapy
25 Rosslyn Avenue
East Barnet
Hertfordshire EN4 8DH
Tel/Fax: 020 8368 8879
email: info@bsmt.org
website: www.bsmt.org

Music and the Deaf
The Media Centre
7 Northumberland Street
Huddersfield HD1 1RL
Tel: 01484 483115
Fax: 01484 483116
email: info@matd.org.uk
website: www.matd.org.uk

Glossary

Asperger Syndrome: a communication disorder that falls within the autism range

Attention Deficit Hyperactivity Disorder/Attention Deficit Disorder (ADHD/ADD): a medical condition in which the child has difficulties with sustaining attention, controlling behaviour and/or controlling his motor activity

Autistic spectrum disorders: a range of language, communication and social disorders

Blissymbolics: a system for communicating with physically disabled people, using abstract symbols

Braille: a communication system of raised dots used by the visually impaired

Cystic fibrosis: a condition mainly affecting the lungs and pancreas, although the liver and sweat glands may also be affected

DES: Department of Education and Science

DfEE: Department for Education and Employment

DfES: Department for Education and Skills

Dycem mats: flexible mats made of material that 'grips' objects placed on them, so preventing slippage

Dyspraxia: a condition affecting the gross and fine motor movements and skills

Eczema: a condition that affects the skin

Elective mutism: a condition where the child is capable of speech but chooses not to communicate in this way

Fine motor skills: refined movements of the hands, thumb and fingers

Grasp and release: a movement involving the finger(s) and thumb where an object is picked up and then placed elsewhere

Gross motor skills: the larger movements of the arms, legs and body

LSA: Learning Support Assistant

Makaton: a signing system for communicating with people who have communication, language or literacy problems

Midline: the vertical line from the top to the bottom of the body, dividing it into the left and right halves

Mutism: see Elective mutism

Myopia: Short-sightedness

Occupational therapist: a professional who works on the child's fine motor skills and self-help skills

Persona dolls: dolls that have various prostheses or equipment for special needs, or that represent different cultures. They are used to help combat discrimination against minorities in our society by presenting them in a positive way

Physiotherapist: a professional who works on the child's gross motor and physical skills

Pinching: the fine motor movements involving the forefinger and thumb

Prophylactic inhaled treatment: medication taken by inhalation as a preventative measure

SENCO: Special Educational Needs Coordinator

Spatial awareness: the ability to recognise our own body and its position in relation to the environment

Velcro: a fastening system comprising two halves of material joined by a 'hook and grasp' method

References and recommended reading

Most of the following books are recommended because of their stimulating and practical ideas and suggestions for activities and games for children with a variety of special educational needs, or because of their usefulness in giving some background to working with special needs children.

Brown, B. (2001) *Combating Discrimination: Persona Dolls in Action.* Stoke-on-Trent: Trentham Books.

Carle, E. (1969) *The Very Hungry Caterpillar.* London: Hamish Hamilton.

Cousins, J. (1999) *Listening to Four-Year-Olds.* London: National Early Years Network.

Department for Education and Employment (DfEE)/Qualifications and Curriculum Authority (QCA) (2000) *Curriculum guidance for the foundation stage.* London: DfEE/QCA.

Department for Education and Skills (DfES) (2001) *Special Educational Needs Code of Practice.* London: DfES.

Dickins, M. and Denziloe, J. (1998) *All together, How to create inclusive services for disabled children and their families: A Practical Handbook for Early Years Workers.* London: National Early Years Network.

Drifte, C. (2001) *Special Needs in Early Years Settings: A Guide for Practitioners.* London: David Fulton Publishers.

Lear, R. (1996) *Play Helps.* Oxford: Heinemann Educational.

Lear, R. (1998) *Look at it This Way.* Oxford: Heinemann Educational.

Lear, R. (1999) *Fingers and Thumbs: Toys and Activities for Children with Hand-function Problems.* Oxford: Butterworth Heinemann.

Lear, R. (2001) *Fun Without Fatigue.* Oxford: Butterworth Heinemann.

Macintyre, C. (2001) *Early Intervention in Movement: Practical Activities for the Early Years Classroom.* London: David Fulton Publishers.

Macintyre, C. (2001) *Enhancing Learning through Play.* London: David Fulton Publishers.

Marl, K. (2000) *The Accessible Games Book.* London: Jessica Kingsley Publishers.

Neaum, S. and Tallack, J. (2000) *Good Practice in Implementing the Pre-school Curriculum.* London: Stanley Thornes.

Roberts, J. (2000) 'The rhetoric must match the practice', *Early Years Educator* **2**(5).

Sayeed, Z. and Guerin, E. (2000) *Early Years Play: A Happy Medium for Assessment and Intervention.* London: David Fulton Publishers.

Seach, D. (1998) *Autistic Spectrum Disorder: Positive Approaches for Teaching Children with ASD.* NASEN.

Umansky, K. (1999) *Nonsense Counting Rhymes.* Oxford: Oxford University Press.

Index